WOODWORKER'S SOURCE BOOK

Also by Charles Self:

Movable Storage Projects
101 Quick & Easy Woodworking Projects
Bricklaying: A Do-It-Yourselfer's Guide
Joinery: Methods of Fastening Wood
Making Pet Houses & Other Projects
Making Fancy Birdhouses & Feeders
Wood Fences & Gates
The Complete Book of Bathrooms
Making Birdhouses & Feeders
Fasten It
Woodworking Tools & Hardware
Kitchen Builder's Handbook
Do Your Own Professional Welding
Wood Heating Handbook, 2nd edition
Country Living
Bathroom Remodeling
Backyard Builder's Bible
Brickworker's Bible
Winning Through Grooming
Western Horsemanship
Working with Plywood
Vacation Home Building
The Brazer's Handbook
Building Your Own Home
Underground Plant Life
Minor Auto Body Repair
Chainsaw Use & Repair
Wood Heating Handbook
Book of Mini-Cycles & Mini-Bikes
How to Take Action Photographs

WOODWORKER'S SOURCE BOOK

CHARLES SELF

BETTERWAY BOOKS
CINCINNATI, OHIO

Book design by Studio 500
Typography by Blackhawk Typesetting

97 96 95 94   5 4 3 2

Library of Congress Cataloging-in-Publication Data

Self, Charles R.
    Woodworker's source book / Charles Self.
      p. cm.
    Includes index.
    ISBN 1-55870-304-7
    1. Woodwork — Equipment and supplies — Directories. 2. Woodwork —
Directories.   I. title.
  TT186.S43 1993
  684'.08'028 — dc20   93-24795
                                                              CIP

CONTENTS

INTRODUCTION

This source book is intended as an up-to-date resource for woodworkers who need to find tools, materials, plans, books, and hundreds of other items. One of the book's main purposes is to allow you to locate items you either know exist or feel must exist somewhere. Otherwise, we aim at providing you a look at a whole slew of things, whether plans or paints, that you may not know exist. Lots of effort has been brought to bear on getting current information for this book, but you should never, ever send off money without checking first that the source's information is still up to date.

I have had a great time going over catalogs, plans, product sheets, course catalogs, and other material. I hope you find a lot of useful and interesting material listed here and then get the same enjoyment out of it. The aim has been to bring you a great deal of information on getting information, products, and supplies that will help you enjoy woodworking more. I believe we have met that aim, and hope you will agree.

SECTION I

❦

USING MAIL ORDER RESOURCES

Buying and selling are long-standing traditions of the human race, ones that will be maintained into the foreseeable future. Within this tradition, we find different characters doing different things — bad reputations abound, and good reputations often don't get as much attention as they deserve. At the same time, we need little protection from businessmen and women with good intentions and repute, and we need solid help in dealing with the few crooked types who exist.

It may generally be said that the selection of tools and supplies of almost all kinds for woodworkers widens by an appreciably large factor when shopping is done by mail. That widening requires both research and caution. Research acquaints you with the variety and quality of products available in that vast marketplace. Caution makes sure you get the best value for your money.

Mail order amongst the woodworking suppliers, whether from makers, retailers, or plans services, is not totally risk free, but is generally better than with other products. Computer shoppers are far too often ripped off by mail order suppliers — though that is easy enough to prevent — who never intend to supply what is sold. This occurs, in part, because the prices are currently (and likely to remain) extremely volatile in the computer field, so ads for spectacular deals are not always seen as rip-offs (and often are *not*). Such seemingly too-good-to-be-true advertisements in other fields are a starting point for avoidance. If it's too good to be true, then it isn't true. Period.

Diamond whetstones are available by mail.
Courtesy of DMT.

I cannot vouch for every company listed in the book. In fact, because of the changing nature of business, I cannot really vouch even for the ones I have dealt with for years. I can state that those I have dealt with have all been honest in filling orders, and as speedy as a realistically filled warehouse allows. The companies I have personally dealt with are often noted in the descriptive material.

START WITH RESEARCH

Start by doing a little research on any mail order company where your expenditures are apt to amount to much: check the company's standing with their local Better Business Bureau. Most of us don't want to bother with this extra work if we are ordering only a few dollars' worth of supplies, but any major tool purchases definitely need at least minimal research to determine how long the company has been in business, whether it has received extensive numbers of complaints, and how it has resolved those complaints. A small number of complaints against a company need not be a point to make you consider avoiding purchasing from them, if they have been in business for some time; the complaint number coincides with BBB's consideration of a typical, or reasonable, human error factor; and the complaints that deserved resolution received it promptly and equitably.

If, as recently happened with a shoe company in my area, complaints have not been quickly resolved, with large numbers going back more than ninety days, keep your money in your wallet, or find another company offering the same products. That shoe company has gone bankrupt — forcibly — and it now seems doubtful customers, some of whom have now waited a year for their product, will see much, if any, in the way of refunds.

USE CREDIT CARDS

Use credit cards when ordering. I am not an aficionado of plastic, because of the obscene interest rates they all charge (including those who charge several percentage points lower than most) added to ludicrous fees. But credit cards give you more protection against fraud, as you can refuse payment if an article is not up to snuff, or is not shipped but is charged. You may refuse payment to the credit card company when there is a dispute with the retailer over costs, quality, or non-supply, and the credit card company cannot make adverse comments to credit bureaus until the situation is resolved. Of course, if it is resolved in your favor, they still may not make adverse comments. Simply put, paying with a credit card allows you much more leeway in backing out of a deal than does paying by check or money order. If ordered material doesn't show up, but a credit card charge does, you do not have to pay that charge. If ordered material is not what was described, you can return items (get a return authorization if the retailer or distributor requires one) without major fiscal penalty, though you may end up paying shipping.

Part of the reason I dislike the usuriously high interest rates (beyond having paid them myself, and noting how long it can take to pay down an account using the monthly minimum payment, while you pay many, many times the cost of the item purchased in interest) is the fact the issuing banks also nail the merchants a rate ranging from a low of over 2% to as much as 6% of the sale cost of an item. Keep an eye out for disclaimers: "The above prices reflect a discount for cash" is an example. Pay by credit card and they can stick you a further percentage, a factor that becomes painful when buying an item like a large table saw. This percentage, whether noted or not, is paid no matter how fast you pay off your credit card. Beat the 12-24% interest blues, and they are still getting you 3-6% additional, whether or not it is listed as surcharge.

Surcharges are illegal in several states (currently California, Florida, Kansas, New York, Connecticut, Maine, Massachusetts, Oklahoma, and Texas), and are against the stated policies of the big three credit card issuers. At the same time, I have paid surcharges on many photographic items ordered from several New York city mail order dealers, and will probably do so again. The reasons are simple: many of the products I order are either not readily available locally, or cost as much as 30% more here than there. A 5% surcharge and an overblown shipping charge appear modest when applied to photo paper, film, and chemicals that still end up costing me about 20 to 25% less than I would otherwise pay.

The same holds true in most mail order fields, though I have not seen surcharges listed in woodworking mail order ads or catalogs.

As noted, the cost may be worth it, for the above reasons. Too, added cost may prove worthwhile because credit cards speed orders: a personal check is not going to get you next day delivery on anything, no matter how badly you need it. In most cases, your check will take several days to clear after it arrives. And a personal check cannot have payment stopped after it has cleared through your account. You can hang up a credit card account on disputed charges.

ORDERING C.O.D.

If a credit card purchase is not an option, order C.O.D. Cash on delivery means you are assured, at minimum, of getting the merchandise, or something similar to the merchandise, before you lay out any money. Pay C.O.D. charges by check, not by money order or with cash. Some companies won't allow check payments, but most will. United Parcel Service

drivers do not like cash C.O.D. payments because cash makes them more vulnerable to robbers.

If the object you ordered is not as described, you can stop payment on the C.O.D. check and sort out the financial hassles by mail and phone later. C.O.D. costs are not cheap, and stopping payment on a check is also costly, but even added up, these charges are better than losing all your money.

Anytime you take unilateral phone action to stop a check, make a complaint, or carry through a promise, it is best to notify the company in writing that you have done so. You then have a record of the proceedings that is a little better than a phone bill with a number and date on it, but make sure you save those phone bills, in case of later dispute over contact dates.

ORDERING ACTIONS

After working through the catalog, brochure, or other literature, write down exactly what you are ordering, including catalog number, description, catalog page number, price, shipping cost, and total, including any state or local tax. Note the date. If you are mailing the order, make a separate copy and file it in your home, or business, files. If you phone in the order, file the remaining copy.

Note on the phoned-in order copy the name of the person you dealt with, any order number that is supplied, and the promised delivery date, plus any added costs.

Like too many people, I have a very bad habit on phone orders, one that I have only recently broken: I seldom wrote down anything more than the item number and description, paid no attention to price, name of order recipient, or

Mail order offers wide lines of tools and accessories.
Courtesy of Irwin.

similar information. The result not long ago was that I received four of an item I had ordered two of, and would have had to do a ridiculous amount of work to return the extra two, ultimately at my own expense for packing and shipping. Fortunately, the items make superb gifts, so I just stuck them in a closet for now. But I might well have found myself out $40, plus shipping, if I had no further use for the material, simply because of human error. (My assumption is the human error, because I have done business with this company a number of times, and found them scrupulously honest and fair). The company would probably have accepted the return, and they might even have credited the shipping costs, but in the process of straightening it all out, I would have lost a couple hours I don't have to spare. The time to correct the error would have been shortened to repacking the extra, with a fast note, if I had kept more order information.

If you have the "Don't write it down, they won't goof" attitude, repair it now.

WHEN YOUR ORDER ARRIVES

When your order arrives, check the outside of the package. If you are dealing with a trucking company, make your notes on the bill of lading before signing your name. Note the size and location of any apparent damage, and sign as taking receipt with recourse if damage also proves internal. Most of the time, with modern packaging, it won't. Large tools are packed in heavy cardboard, and very large tools have wooden supports in the cardboard. Smaller items are usually thoroughly surrounded with Styrofoam or similar material. Protection in the packaging is excellent, but truly rough handling may damage things anyway. Check. Let both the shipping company and the selling company know immediately if there is damage.

When you open the package, check the contents against your order list. If everything is in good condition and matches the list, most of the time your chores come close to an end here. Check the packing slip for costs. If you have paid in full, by credit card or other means, it should be so noted. Next, fill out any warranty cards and return them to the indicated addresses, keeping a copy of the card and the address to which it is sent. (I have gotten some warranty cards that don't even have the name of the manufacturer on them: note the maker's name if that is the case.)

Actually, I like to go an extra step. Assemble all items that need assembly, and take a test run through with any tools before mailing in the warranty cards. Many years ago, I bought a new camera, unpacked it, tossed the packing material, and mailed in the warranty card. I then used the camera to shoot a roll of film, which I should have done

before shipping off the card or destroying the packaging. The camera was defective, and I ended up having to trade it back to the dealer as used. I felt I was ripped off and I was, so I never dealt with that dealer again, but I also let myself in for the problems by discarding the packaging and mailing the warranty card prematurely. The dealer had to go through a longer process to get the camera either repaired or replaced, and there was no way it looked new when it got back there. A better dealer would have worked with me to replace the defective unit, but this one got snotty, I got angry in return, and I ended up with a much more costly camera (that I used happily for fifteen years), heartburn, and absolute delight when, three years later, the dealer went belly up.

PROBLEMS WITH THE ORDER

If you have problems with a match to the list or with broken items, your work begins. Don't follow my example above with the camera dealer. The first rule is to keep your cool. Get all your paperwork in front of you. If necessary, write some notes on the problem. Then call the dealer.

From this point, you will deal at least partly in luck. Today, most mail order dealers work on the "Satisfaction Guaranteed" basis introduced a million years ago by Sears, Roebuck. People handling the phones are instructed that customer is always and forever right, even if the customer comes across as a drooling fumblewit. (They are instructed to hang up on abusive customers, so going hog wild does no one any good.)

Explain the problem, and expect a responsive reply, or a transfer to a supervisor who can provide a substantive response. If such a response isn't forthcoming, you will want to move up a step within the company, if possible. If it isn't possible, make sure you have the name of the person with whom you have been talking, and explain that you will next be providing their name, the company's name and address, and details of the problem to their local Better Business Bureau.

Follow up on your promise by writing a reasoned letter detailing the problem, mailing it to the company's local BBB (you can get its address from your BBB), and mailing copies of your letter to the company as well.

If you feel you have been defrauded, the next step is to take your complaint to the postal authorities. Though very little mail order is really done through the mails today, a great deal of other company business is conducted that way — and a fairly large number of people still use the mail, instead of the phone, to order. The threat of action is often enough to solve the problem ... if you make a reasoned case, presented with clear details.

The Japan Woodworker's array of some of its items shows mail order at its best. Very few local stores can offer such a selection.

The preceding seems to make a gray, gray case for mail order. It shouldn't. For every poorly handled transaction, there must be at least several hundred that are handled pleasantly and efficiently. But with the cost of some tools today, it pays to know your options just in case something goes wrong. Protecting yourself takes only a moment or two. It will probably never be needed, but is, like most insurance, a great mind easer.

Section II

Distributors, Importers, and Manufacturers

3M DIY DIVISION

Consumer Relations
515-3N-02
St. Paul MN 55144-1000

This is the 3M division that handles information on Newstroke snap-off paint brushes, home care adhesives, and surface prep products (hand and power sanding materials), paint removers, and personal safety products, such as goggles and face masks of both comfort and respirator types. You can request catalogs, but be specific as to which product lines interest you, then go ahead and request the catalogs. There are several different catalogs, one for each product line.

A.R.E. MANUFACTURING, INC.

518 S. Springbrook Rd.
Newberg OR 97132   (800) 541-4962

The Correct Cut radial arm saw fence replaces the existing fence, provides a precise measuring scale, and has a built-in hinged stop. It is available in any length. Call or write for further information.

ACCUSET TOOL COMPANY

P.O. Box 1088   (800) 343-6129
Troy MI 48099   (313) 879-0030

Paraguage for setting tool fences.

ADAMS WOOD PRODUCTS

974 Forest Dr.   (615) 587-2942
Morristown TN 37814   FAX: (615) 586-2188

The free Adams catalog shows legs for projects from Queen Anne to tapered in enough detail to make me wish one of my current or immediately upcoming projects needed such legs. Stock items include Queen Anne legs, table bases, table and chair kits, in walnut, cherry, oak, mahogany, and maple. Carved knees may be added to many Queen Anne legs, as may claw and ball feet. Bun and tapered feet are also available. Prices vary widely, depending on your needs. Obviously, more costly woods mean more costly parts, as do longer and larger parts. Leg length varies from 8" to 29½", with a box of forty-eight for the smaller legs and a box of a dozen for the longer. Part box prices are the highest, so if you foresee using a dozen long legs over the years, buy the box and save a bit over 10 percent. Turned table legs are less costly until you get into fluted types, of which Adams Wood Products carries a wide variety.

The catalog is interesting, and the idea of not having to bandsaw Queen Anne-style legs makes the prices very reasonable. Overall, the products open out the project possibilities for those of us without bandsaws and lathes. Oak table columns and feet are available too, and some items may now be made of mesquite.

ADJUSTABLE CLAMP COMPANY

415 N. Ashland Ave.
Chicago IL 60622

One of the oldest wide line clamp manufacturers, Adjustable Clamp Company makes Jorgenson and Pony clamps, in styles ranging from light, heavy, and medium bar clamps to C clamps to spring clamps, with virtually every stop in between. At this time, I believe they are also the only U.S. maker of handscrews. Write for free "Clamp-It" brochure.

ADVANCED MACHINERY IMPORTS

2 McCullough Dr.
P.O. Box 312   (800) 648-4264
New Castle DE 19720   (302) 322-2226

Along with the Plano Vertical Glue System, AMI offers Hegner scroll saws. Information on their products is available for a phone call or postcard.

AIRSTREAM DUST HELMETS

Hwy. 54 South   (800) 328-1792
P.O. Box 975   (218) 685-4457
Elbow Lake MN 56531   FAX: (218) 685-4458

Airstream is the distributor for the Racal line of lung and eye protection helmets — respirators — that provide protection

The Airstream Airmate 3 helmet.

from dust, lacquers, glues, and strippers. The company also distributes hearing protectors, safety glasses, and a negative (no air pump) respirator for those who don't wish to pay the cost of the positive (pumped air) systems. Catalogs are available at no charge, on request. Airstream sells through its own mail order company.

The Airstream Airmate 1 face shield and hat.

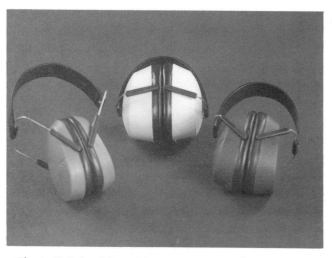

Classic "Mickey Mouse" hearing protectors from Airstream. Good quality hearing protection is an essential that I wish had been available when I first began working with power tools.

AMERICAN CLAMPING CORPORATION

P.O. Box 399
Batavia NY 14021   (800) 828-1004

ACC imports Bessey clamps, which include the K body heavy cabinet clamps, the best I have ever used, and lines of light to heavy bar clamps, specialty clamps, and others. Write or call for free literature.

AMERICAN MACHINE & TOOL COMPANY

Fourth Ave. and Spring St.   (215) 948-0400
Royersford PA 19468-2519   FAX: (215) 948-5300
                                   Orders: (800) 435-8665
Customer service, parts, inquiries: (800) 435-3279

American Machine & Tool Company distributes tools made for it in Taiwan. The AMT line of low to moderate cost tools and their range of accessories is shown in a free catalog. Over time, I have used AMT lathes and drill presses, plus a number of accessories, and found them excellent representatives of the moderate part of the price scale for power tools. I have not had a chance to use their newer lines of hand tools and accessories, but expect that they will be on a par with the other lines. The drill press accepts a wide variety of accessories, all also sold by AMT.

AMERICAN TOOL COMPANIES

P.O. Box 337
DeWitt NE 68341   (402) 683-2315

Quick-Grip clamps are the tools for woodworker's choice from the makers of Vise Grips, but American Tool also

Chesco's fold-up tool set is handy around any shop.

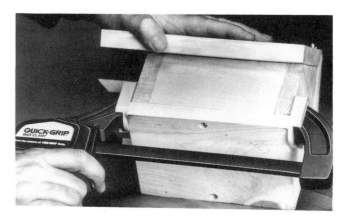

Quick-Grip clamps from American Tool Company go from small to large (36" is the maximum size available).

manufactures Pro Snips, Chesco hex tools, Unibits (a multi-sized sheet metal bit), and a variety of other tools. For those who haven't used them, Quick-Grip clamps are real timesavers and well worth investigating if you do any kind of woodworking that calls for bar clamps.

ANDREW SHIMANOFF TOOL DESIGNS

P.O. Box 1318
Ashland OR 97520   (503) 488-3059

Shimanoff's woodturner's Steady Rest for lathe work is designed to speed up and ease spindle turning. A free brochure shows details and gives ordering information; $2.00 will get you an informative how-to booklet that also includes turning tips.

ANGLEWRIGHT TOOL COMPANY

P.O. Box 25632
Los Angeles CA 90025   (310) 471-7432

The AngleWright is a table saw miter gauge tool that is rugged, accurate within 1/10 of a degree, and easy to use. Call or write for a free brochure.

ARROW FASTENER COMPANY

271 Mayhill St.
Saddle Brook NJ 07662

Arrow makes a wide line of staplers, both manual and electric, and staples. Write for information on the product lines.

ATLAS COPCO ELECTRIC TOOLS INC.

3 Shaw's Cove   (800) 243-0870
New London CT 06320   FAX: (203) 447-4624

Atlas Copco markets the AEG line of power tools, a complete line of power hand tools, from nibblers through circular saws, and including corded and cordless drills, hammer-drills, slide compound miter saws, random orbit sanders (including a unique, to me at least, cordless model), belt sanders, and more. Their cordless line is a more extensive than most, right up to and including caulking and adhesive guns. AEG chooses to call their battery-powered models "cordfree." A mini-catalog and price list is free for a phone call or a card.

AUTON COMPANY

Box 1129   (818) 367-4340
Sun Valley CA 91353   FAX: (818) 362-9215

Auton pop-up TV lifts are great for hiding television sets in good-looking cabinets. Write or call for information.

BALL AND BALL

463 W. Lincoln Hwy.
Exton PA 19341   (215) 363-7330

The Ball and Ball reproduction hardware catalog is $5.00 (108 pages), but they will send a free mini-catalog on request.

BEALL TOOL CO.

541 Swans Rd. NE   (800) 331-4718
Newark OH 43055   (614) 345-5045

The Beall wood threader for router use comes in three left-hand and five right-hand sizes. It is one of the tools I have not yet used, and one that I am itching to try. To add to my itch, Judith Beall sent along a copy of their *The Nuts & Bolts of Woodworking*, with twenty projects and a huge quantity of information. Write or call for a very informative brochure. Distribution is nearly worldwide, and Beall also sells direct.

The AEG cordless drill is primarily available through mail order. Courtesy of Atlas Copco Electric Tools, Inc.

Chiseling out a mortise with mail order tools. Photo by the author.

BELWITH

18071 Arenth Ave.
P.O. Box 8430   (818) 965-5533
City of Industry CA 91748   (800) 235-9484

Cabinet and box hardware covering a wide range is shown in their $4.75 catalog.

BETTER BUILT CORPORATION

845 Woburn St.
Wilmington MA 01887   (508) 657-5636

Makers of the RipSaw portable sawmill, Better Built offers a free brochure describing the one-man bandsaw mill that cuts logs to 20" diameter, providing boards up to 9" thick and 14" wide.

BIESEMEYER MANUFACTURING

(800) 782-1831

This company manufactures one of the top-of-the-line aftermarket table saw fences. Call for free information and may your luck be better than mine. My request seems to have gotten lost, but I have occasionally used and very much liked the product so am including a mention.

BILL BARTZ MANUFACTURING COMPANY

854 Arbor Oaks Dr.   (707) 451-9104
Vacaville CA 95687   (707) 451-4666

Bill's MitreRite costs $19.95 plus $3.00 shipping, and it works. It's a simple device — a series of devices, really — of plastic, including a tool for making four-sided frames, another for making six-sided frames, and a third that works for eight-sided frames, circles, and ovals. In essence, it is a flip-over guide that fits in front of the miter gauge on a table

DIY Retailing award is for Bill Bartz's MitreRite.

saw. (It works, with a minor procedure change, with radial arm saws too.) The only requirement for table saws is that the miter gauge slots be parallel to the saw blade, which is a standard setup need in any case. The MitreRite then produces complementary angles, so that you have a good fit. One cut is made, the miter gauge and guide moved to the other gauge slot, and the second cut is made after flipping the guide over. Any deviation from an accurately angled cut is made up for when the gauge is moved and the guide flipped, so you get gap-free joints. The MitreRite won the Retailer's Choice Award at the National Hardware Show in August of 1992.

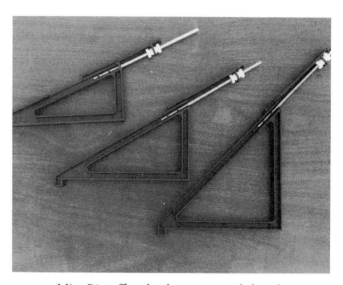

MitreRite offers the three most needed angles.

BLACK & DECKER (U.S.), INC.

Power Tool Div.
P.O. Box 798
Hunt Valley MD 21030

Write for the Black & Decker consumer line catalog of one of the widest and most popular lines of portable power tools made.

BORDEN

Home & Professional Products Group
180 E. Broad St.
Columbus OH 43215-3799   (800) 848-9400

Borden's line of wood glues, white glues, and specialty adhesives can be of great help to woodworkers. One of their most useful products around the shop is Elmer's Carpenter's Wood Glue for Darker Woods. This glue is great for the person who works a lot with cherry, mahogany, walnut, and similar dark woods because the glue line comes closer to matching the color of the wood. As an aliphatic resin adhesive, it resists gum-up from friction (no balling up during

Black & Decker's Elu line is aimed at the advanced woodworker.

Black & Decker's 10" bench-top table saw.

Black & Decker's Piranha blades come ready for rough or fine cutting.

A new addition is Black & Decker's 10" bench-top bandsaw. Bench-top tools are having a new surge in popularity for those with limited workshop space or funds or both.

sanding). Of course, the Elmer's line includes Glue-All, one of the most successful of the white (polyvinyl) resin glues. Borden's Elmer's line includes contact cements, caulks, silicone seals, Krazy Glue, threadlockers, rubber cement, a multitude of colored glues intended for school children, and similar items.

BOSCH POWER TOOL CORP.

100 Bosch Blvd.
New Bern NC 28562   (800) 334-4151

Bosch tools have a tremendous reputation for quality but tend to be a little hard to find outside a few catalogs. The

Bosch's orbital action dustless jig saw is one of the best manufactured.

Bosch offers this entry in the random orbit sander race.

company makes a full line of portable power tools, from circular saws and drills, on to routers, jig saws, cordless drills, and screwdrivers, random orbit as well as belt and sheet sanders, and more. The tools are getting easier to find and may become easier by far in the near future as Skil takes a part in distribution of the tools. Call for a free catalog and the address of local dealerships.

BOSSWORKS

4510 W. 77th St.
Suite 239   (612) 496-4297
Minneapolis MN 55435   FAX: (612) 831-4186

WoodBoss Acrylic Clear Wood Sealant is an exterior wood protector that is sprayed (low-pressure spraying such as with a garden sprayer is recommended) and provides good protection for such exterior projects as Adirondack chairs and almost any kind of lawn and garden furniture or similar projects.

BRANDMARK BY

F&K Concepts
462 Carthage Dr.   (800) 323-2570
Beavercreek OH 45434-5865   (513) 426-6843

The project branding iron produced by F&K Concepts, and called BrandMark, is available in several styles. The simplest is the type heated with a torch or hot plate and costs $28.00. The electric branding iron is more complex and costs $48.00. Either iron gives you a chance to quickly and permanently mark all your completed projects. The standard first line says: Handcrafted By. The second line can have up to twenty spaces, with a ¼" letter height. The first line can be changed, and third and fourth lines and special figures may all be added at extra cost.

BrandMark project brander is by F&K.

LARRY & FAYE BRUSSO COMPANY

3812 Cass-Elizabeth
Waterford MI 48328   (313) 682-4320

The Brussos produce exceptionally fine solid brass hardware for custom cabinetry and fine boxes. All hardware is machined from solid brass stock, hand fitted and finished nicely, to produce show quality hinges. I have recently built a walnut hope chest using their hinges and find them truly exceptional. I suggest checking prices directly, because brass stock is fluctuating at press time. Brusso hinges are sold by many of the mail order firms, and are available directly in quantities of ten and up. Call or write for a retail price schedule.

CALCULATED INDUSTRIES

22720 Savi Ranch   (714) 921-1800
Yorba Linda CA 92687   (800) 854-8075
                      FAX: (714) 921-2799

The Construction Master II feet-inch calculator adds, subtracts, and divides in feet and inches, and with any fraction, from ½ to 1/64, including mixed fractions. The CMII will also convert between feet-inch fractions, decimal feet, inches, yards, and metrics, including square and cubic measurements. With all of this, the CMII also works as a standard math calculator, with many functions, including square roots and auto shut-off. The company distributes and sells direct and accepts credit cards.

CAMPBELL-HAUSFELD

100 Production Dr.
Harrison OH 45030   (800) 634-4793

Campbell-Hausfeld is a leading manufacturer of air compressors, including oilless models. In addition, they have

This is Campbell-Hausfeld's HVLP (high volume, low pressure) spray tool. It looks a little odd when placed alongside a standard high pressure unit and compressor but is very easy to use.

recently come out with a high-volume low-pressure spray kit that is lower in price than industrial versions, and works very nicely in applying clear and other finishes. Campbell-Hausfeld also makes a line of compressed air nailers and staplers, for applications from heavy framing to fabric stapling. Ask for free brochures.

Campbell-Hausfeld's 2½" finish nailer is a sure aid for nail and glue projects and may save lots of assembly and clamping time.

CAPE FORGE

P.O. Box 987
Burlington VT 05402

This small company success story is unusual in that the Cape Forge is a father and ... but not father and son. Mike De Punte has as an apprentice his daughter Karyn, who has a B.A. in Industrial Education and Technology. Karyn turns the hardwood handles for the tools and attends to the fit and finish. Mike forges the blades. From the photos Karyn sent,

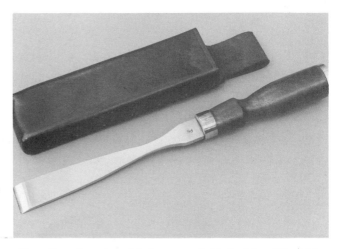

Cape Forge's paring chisels are available in 1" to 2" widths.

the tools are obviously beautifully made. Most of their tools are for carvers and sculptors, but they do make paring chisels that I can hope to get, in at least one or two sizes, in the future. The catalog is $1.00.

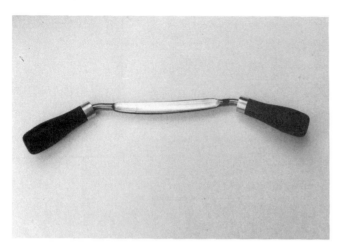

Cape Forge's draw knives come with 5" or 6" blades.

Cape Forge offers a nice two-knife carver's set in a leather case.

CARR LANE MANUFACTURING CO.

4200 Carr Lane Court
P.O. Box 191970   (314) 647-6200
St. Louis MO 63119-2196   FAX: (314) 647-5736

Call or write for free literature on the Carr Lane line of toggle clamps.

CARTER PRODUCTS COMPANY, INC.

437 Spring St. NE   (616) 451-2928
Grand Rapids MI 49503   FAX: (616) 451-4330

For those of us who have trouble keeping bandsaw blades from twisting in their guides, and who have guides that wear

out in days instead of years, Carter produces ball bearing guides that greatly aid precision. These guides are not low cost, though not outrageous. In my experience, they are worth their price, especially on lower cost bandsaws. Carter also produces bandsaw tires and wheels, and a laser guideline light. Free brochures are available on all these products, and others that are probably beyond the interest of hobby woodworkers — lights for woodworking specialties, and a Flip-Pod system to work with CNC production router setups.

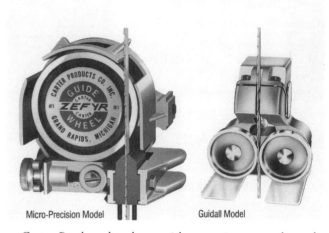

Micro-Precision Model   Guidall Model

Carter Products bandsaw guides come in two grades and work very nicely indeed.

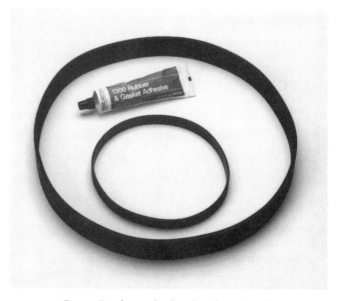

Carter Products also has bandsaw tire kits.

CASCADE TOOLS, INC.

P.O. Box 3110
Bellingham WA 98227   (800) 235-0272

Cascade Tools imports and distributes the SY line of carbide tools, primarily router bits and shaper cutters. There are many unusual items in both arrays, plus some items such as anti-kickback devices, knife-setting jigs, rub collars, dust collection connectors, router bases, roller brackets, and more, including books and videos, and air nailers (brad models) and staplers. The catalog is free and the 800 number takes orders twenty-four hours a day.

Cascade Tools offers decorative router bits.

Cascade Tools also sells specialty router bit sets.

CHANNELLOCK, INC.

1306 S. Main St.
Meadville PA 16335   (814) 724-8700

Channellock is one company that doesn't require much product description. They designed and produced the original pliers based on resizing the jaw opening with channels on the tool neck. In recent years, the tool has been improved, and the line of pliers has been expanded to include nut drivers, slip joint pliers, end nippers, wire cutters of many types, linemen's and electrician's pliers, long nose pliers, aviation (metal) snips, wiring tools and strippers, adjustable wrenches, and a couple of knives. Write and request their free brochures for further information.

CLAYTON ENTERPRISES

2505 W. Dewey Rd.
Owosso MI 48867

Write for free information on Clayton oscillating spindle sanders.

CMT

5425 Beaumont Center Blvd.   U.S.: (800) 531-5559
Tampa FL 33634   Canada: (800) 387-7005

Premium router bits are featured in CMT's free catalog. Sets are available — for Incra, JoinTech, Leigh, OmniJig, and Keller jigs. Call for the catalog.

COLONIAL SAW

100 Pembroke St.
P.O. Box A
Kingston MA 02364   (617) 585-4364

Write or call for free information on biscuits and biscuit hinges.

CONNECTICUT VALLEY MANUFACTURING

P.O. Box 1957
New Britain CT 06050   (203) 223-0076

Convalco Forstner bits are among the best of the type available and they are made in America. Write or call for further information.

CONOVER

Lathe Division
American Woodcraft Tools, Inc.   (800) 722-5447
10420 Kinsman Rd.   (216) 564-9600
Newbury OH 44065   FAX: (216) 564-9566

The Conover lathes are justly famous, using as a base a 16" bed design and partial kits to produce a lathe with an unlimited length. Call for a free catalog.

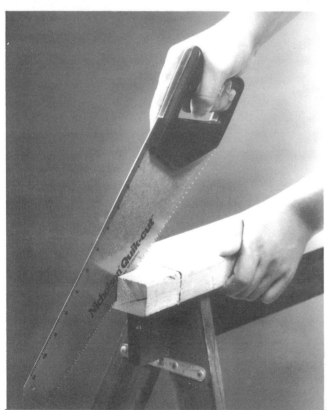

Nicholson's 15" Quik-Cut Short Saw uses an 8 point specialty bevel tooth set, sharpened on both sides for fast cutting, and for use as both a crosscut and ripsaw.

COOPERTOOLS

Box 728
Apex NC 27502   (919) 362-7510

Call or drop a line for free brochures on CooperTools varied lines. For those not already familiar with these top lines, they include Plumb (hammers and similar tools), Nicholson (hand saws, saw blades, files, et al.), Lufkin (measuring tools), Crescent (adjustable wrenches, of course, but also screwdrivers, pliers, and other tools), Wiss (scissors, knives, metal snips), Xcelite (small pliers and cutters and electronic assembly and disassembly tools), Weller (soldering tools), H.K. Porter (cable and chain cutters), Turner (propane torches), Campbell (chain, padlocks), and Covert (pulleys, swivels, and similar accessories).

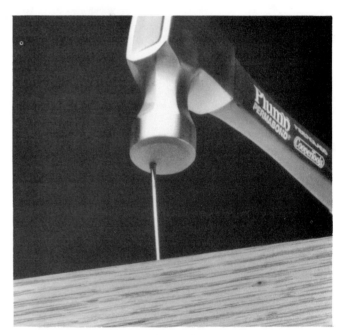

CooperTools new rough-faced Plumb carpenter's hammer doesn't slip even when nails are slightly mis-hit.

CREATIVE TECHNOLOGIES, INC.

300 Phillips Rd.
N. Little Rock AR 72117

This company markets do-it-yourself home siding kits and offers a kit and hand tools catalog for $3.00.

CREDO

2765 National Way
Woodburn OR 97071   (503) 982-0100

Credo presents a variety of saw blades, drill bits, and driver bits. Credo has a specific line of energy-efficient blades and bits and sanding sheets produced for cordless tools, to lengthen working time per charge. The circular saw blades are thin kerf (the saw body is .035") and are said to provide 50% lower battery drain than do conventional blades. Titanium nitride is used as a coating to reduce drag and wear for other bits for cordless tools. Credo also offers a range of standard carbide circular saw blades, spade bits, twist drill bits, and masonry drill bits. Call or drop a note for free color brochures.

D.C. PRECISION TOOLS, INC.

11 Mathews Ave.
Riverdale NJ 07457 (800) 462-2481

Call for information on the Saw-Mate fence-mounted stock pusher for table saws.

DAP, INC.

P.O. Box 277 (800) 543-3840
Dayton OH 45401-0277 (513) 667-4461

Weldwood adhesives work on all sorts of materials and offer some unique properties, such as extreme water resistance, changing dilution for different uses, and more. Call for further information.

DARWORTH COMPANY

3 Mill Pond Lane (800) 672-3499
P.O. Box 639 (800) 624-7767
Simsbury CT 06070 FAX: (800) 227-6095

FI:X Wood Patch and Touch Up Stik are two major products for repair and construction. The color Touch Up Stiks

FI:X Touch Up Stiks offer easy cover-up of mars.

Birch fir FI:X wood patch, from Darworth Company.

do minor touchup jobs in a hurry, while the wood patch is made in red oak, white pine, ash, maple/alder, white, walnut, natural, pine, oak, dark mahogany/redwood, light mahogany, and birch fir. Call or write for further information.

DE-STA-CO.

P.O. Box 2800 (313) 589-2008
Troy MI 48007 (800) 245-2759
FAX: (313) 644-3929

A leading maker of toggle clamps, De-Sta-Co. offers a free catalog of over 300 models. This type of clamp is suitable for most woodworking jigs and fixtures and allows development of new jigs to aid in your workshop. The catalog is very specific in providing measurements of the clamps and their movements and mounting needs. De-Sta-Co also makes a wide line of pneumatic air clamps designed to work on shop line pressure. This is not a usual hobby woodworking application and really is not very often seen in small commercial shops, but it can be a great boon for certain types of wide area work, such as laminating large sheets.

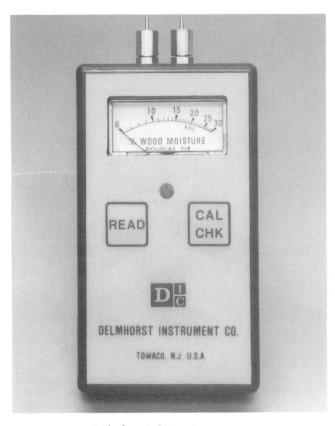

Delmhorst's J-3 moisture meter.

DELMHORST INSTRUMENT COMPANY

51 Indian Lane East   (800) 222-0638
Towaco NJ 07082   In NJ: (201) 334-2557

Delmhorst moisture meters make up the second major line of such meters and include a number of models that cover most aspects of testing wood for moisture. For more information than the illustrations of the individual models shown, give the company a call or drop them a line. I have used the mid-range Delmhorst and find it an excellent and accurate measuring tool.

Delmhorst's J-88 moisture meter.

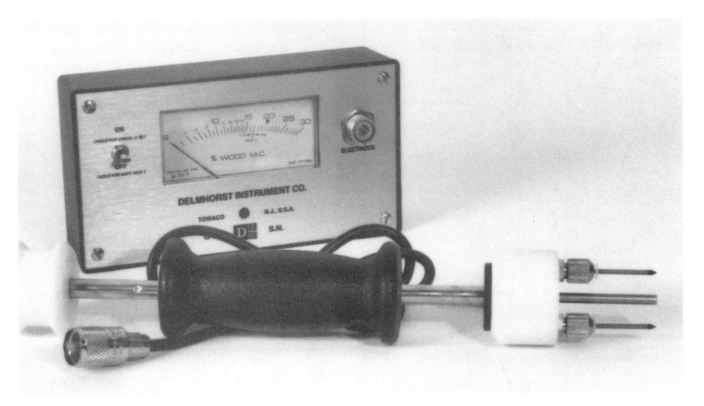

Delmhorst's G-30 with 26-ES electrodes is their top of the line.

DELTA INTERNATIONAL MACHINERY CORP.

(800) 438-2486

The line of Delta power tools includes the Unisaw table saw and the scroll saw illustrated here. There are now two basic Delta lines, with building trades and home shop machinery lines paired in a catalog, which you will find at your dealer (check when you call for the name of your nearest dealer, for the catalog policy may differ). Tools built for contractors and home shop use may differ in some respects (usually being lighter and less costly than industrial machines, but not always, no one can class the 12" 33-890 radial arm saw as light, or less accurate, except possibly those using the huge industrial machines). Delta also offers an 18" 3 phase, 7½ horse unit that is 745 pounds, which is enough and then some. The home shop machinery catalog is a great deal of fun and offers just about anything most of us can want, or come close to affording.

The industrial machinery catalog, as noted above, offers truly heavy-duty machinery for the huge jobs where dead-on accuracy is a must on a day-in, day-out basis. For example, the biggest planer in the home machinery catalog is a 13" (not portable), but Delta's biggest planer is a 24". Delta continually brings out new models, including their Sidekick frame and trim saw (rod-guided compound miter saw, with a cut width of 12" at 90 degrees) and a new dust collector/sweeper. One of the top three American (two U.S., one Canadian) stationary tool makers, Delta will send you a copy of their Building Trades and Home Shop catalog for $1.00.

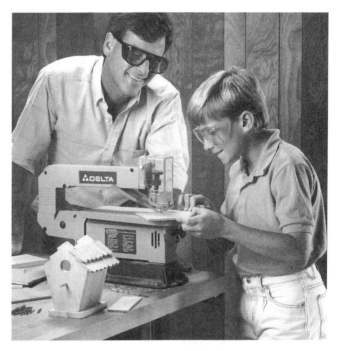

Delta now markets a consumer level scroll saw, in addition to its larger and more costly models.

DELTA TECHNICAL COATINGS, INC.

2550 Pellissier Place   (800) 423-4135
Whittier CA 90601   In CA: (800) 553-8940
                                         (213) 686-0678

Hallmark Home Decor Antiquing Gel is one of Delta's Home Decor line of water-based stains and finishes. Gel wood stain, liquid wood stain, pickling gel, antiquing gel, neutral gel, transparent pearl glaze gel, gel stain retarder, and an acrylic paint base coat make up most of the line. To make it possible to go from the wood out with the same compat-

Delta's Unisaw is here being used with the Unifence and table, which gives much increased capacity for rips and also increased accuracy and ease of handling.

This lovely blanket chest shows what can be done with Delta Technical Coatings products.

ible product line, Home Decor products include wood sealer, dimensional stain resist (used to mask areas to be left unstained), water-based interior varnish in matte, satin, and gloss, an exterior gloss varnish, and wood filler. Products are generally available in two- and eight-ounce containers. Give them a call and request details.

Hallmark Home Decor pickling gel being applied. Courtesy of Delta Technical Coatings.

DEROSE & COMPANY

Box 150   (804) 746-1705
Mechanicsville VA 23111   FAX: (804) 746-2556

This manufacturer of custom lathes offers features that will make a woodturner's mouth water, or hands try to grasp the nearest turning tool. The basic unit has a swing of 25" or 30", with a sliding, rotating head stock (rotation is for outboard turning). The distance between centers can range from 42" (or less) to 102", which is more than sufficient for general use, including bed post turning, unless you must have a bed post longer than 8½'. Information on the DeRose lathe and its options, including lengths greater than 102", can be had for a phone call or a card.

DEVCON CONSUMER DIVISION

A.E.C. Dr.   (800) 227-7950
Wood Dale IL 60191   (708) 350-2710

Devcon makes epoxy and other adhesives of value to the woodworker. Write for information on the lines.

DEVILBISS AIR POWER COMPANY

213 Industrial Dr.   (901) 423-7000
Jackson TN 38301   FAX: (901) 423-7900

The DeVilbiss line of Air America compressors runs the gamut from a small ¾ horse oilless model that you can almost tuck in your back pocket (it takes a big pocket, but weighs only 14 pounds, without a tank, and 25 with) to a monster 5 horse two-stage industrial model that delivers 175 PSI and weighs 413 pounds. In between, there are Air America models for almost every do-it-yourself or commercial use, with tools to accompany the compressors. DeVilbiss lists spray guns, air ratchets, dual-action circular sanders, air impact wrenches, air chisels, air staplers, jitterbug air sanders, paint tanks, blow guns, and other tools to go with the Air America line of compressors. Naturally, the compressors will drive finish nailers and similar tools from other makers. Write for free brochures.

DIANSUPPLY/LABORSABER COMPANY

4505 Green Park Rd.   (800) 331-6480
St. Louis MO 63123   (314) 892-8597
                                 FAX: (314) 892-6814

Diansupply/Laborsaber Company will provide a free packet of information on their new economy-priced professional model retractable scroll saw that works from the bottom up.

DMT

85 Hayes Memorial Dr.   (508) 481-5944
Marlborough MA 01752   FAX: (508) 485-3924

Router and shaper bit sharpening stones make up the product list of this manufacturer. Diamond Machining

Diamond Whetstones are designed to work perfectly on many bit shapes and types. Courtesy of Diamond Machining Technology.

Technology manufactures a wide and unique line of sharpening stones in shapes to fit just about any tool. DMT has Diamond Whetstones, Diamond Sanding Disks, Diamond Honing Cones, and others, in grits ranging from a rough (extra-coarse) 220 for fast stock removal, to 1200 for giving a tool that final hone and polish. Ask for their free product user brochure, and check on catalog availability. Most of their product line is sold by top mail order suppliers.

DOVER PUBLICATIONS, INC.

31 East 2nd St.
Mineola NY 11501

Dover's catalog is free and lists many woodworking titles and related titles, from old to new. At one time, Dover published only reprints, but in recent years they have gone to publishing more and more new material, while retaining the lead in publishing old crafts (and other) material. They have books on wood turning, for example, that go back centuries to provide plentiful examples of how it was done, with some help toward getting it done today if you apply some study and thought. Always an interesting book, the Dover catalog in recent years has turned more into a series of catalogs on different subjects, plus a full line catalog. Ask for the full line catalog, just in case.

DREMEL

4915 21st St.
Racine WI 53406

Dremel is the manufacturer of the Moto-Tool in all its variations and with all its companion tools. The free Dremel catalog lists six versions of the Moto-Tool, a Moto-Flex tool, accessories, and bits galore. Shortly after, you find the Moto-Shop scroll saw/sander and its accessories, which leads on to a disc-belt sander, a 4" tilt arbor table saw, a miniature lathe, a shoe polisher, glue guns, lights, chainsaw sharpening tools, wood-burning kits, and many, many plans. All of these are available at your dealer or may be ordered.

DYNAMAT

1140 Lakeland Dr. N #101   (800) 800-2038
Minneapolis MN 55369   FAX: (612) 429-4399

Dynamat is the maker of anti-fatigue mats that provide industrial quality for the home workshop. The polyvinyl chloride mats are 24" x 36" x 3/8" thick, and resist water, oil, detergents, and sawdust. The mats make concrete floors a great deal easier on one's back, and retail for about $19.00.

EBAC LUMBER DRYERS

106 John Jefferson Rd.   (800) 433-9011
Suite 102   (804) 229-3038
Williamsburg VA 23185   FAX: (804) 229-3321

For the heavy wood user, Ebac presents three lumber dryer systems that sell for under $3,000, with systems perfected to the point where no experience is needed to get perfectly dried lumber. An example is the TR250, which works on loads from 50 to 250 board feet, drying lumber to 6 to 8% moisture content (recommended cabinet-making range). The buyer builds the kiln chamber, which is one reason the price is within reason. Call or write for further information.

Ebac's TR250 dryer unit and control panel. You build the actual oven, to sizes that will fit almost anywhere.

EDWARD J. BENNETT COMPANY

Fair Oaks Industrial Park
1016 Morse Ave.
Suite 21   (800) 333-4994
Sunnyvale CA 94089   (408) 744-0179

The TS-Aligner for table saws is a dial alignment gauge that will rapidly show whether or not the blade is parallel to the rip fence. Call or write for further information.

ELECTROPHYSICS

Box 1143, Station B
London ONT
Canada N6A 5K2   (519) 668-2871

Eight models of wood moisture meters for home or industrial uses. Call or write for free catalog.

EMPEROR CLOCK COMPANY

Emperor Industrial Park
Fairhope AL 36532   (205) 928-2316

Emperor's clock kits and furniture kits come in solid oak and cherry and let you furnish your home at a fraction of the cost of already built furniture, before you develop all the skills required for full-scale, complex woodworking. All parts are pre-cut, and the frames and doors have already been assembled. The color catalog is $1.00.

EXCALIBUR

210 Eighth St. S.
Lewiston NY 14092 (800) 387-9789

The Excalibur T slot saw fence, with its various accessories, is a reasonably easy to install replacement and upgrade unit for table saws. I used one for years on my Delta Unisaw and found it met every claim made for it. Accessories include a router table to be built into the saw fence extension table, router fence brackets, a stock pusher, and guide rail work stops. Two stock guide rail lengths are available, allowing rip cuts to the right of the blade of 33" and 62"; and two fence lengths, for different size saw tables, are available. Excalibur makes its own sliding table for table saws, allowing excellent crosscut accuracy to go with the T-slot fence's great rip cut accuracy. For those who have not used them, sliding tables on stationary saws add fantastic cutting abilities and accuracy, if well made. The Excalibur comes in two sizes, the EXSLT30, giving a 28" crosscut depth (to the front of a 10" blade); and the EXSLT60, with a crosscut depth of 37". Excalibur also offers an over-arm blade cover for dust collection. More information is available from Excalibur.

EXCALIBUR MACHINE CORP.

P.O. Box 82
Anderson MO 64831 (800) 368-ROSS

Excalibur will send a free brochure on the Ross drum sander, a wide drum stationary model that competes with several other large sanders. Several widths are listed, including 26" and 37", both with feed rates adjustable from 0 to 14½ feet per minute. Both are available with single phase power, though the 37" model comes standard with a 10 horse three phase unit, and must step down to a 7½ horse motor to work on single phase power. Power table lifts are available and are said to help considerably on large models. Smaller units are available and less costly than the huge models. Write or call for a brochure, or send $9.95 (refundable) plus $2.00 shipping (U.S.: Send $16.95 Canadian) for a videotape of the 12", 26", and 37" machines in operation.

FARRIS MACHINERY

309 N. 10th
Blue Springs MO 64015 (800) USA-KITY

As you might guess from the phone number, Farris Machinery imports the KITY K5, a multi-machine that has a 10" table saw, a 6" jointer, a thickness planer, a ¾" spindle shaper, and a mortiser. The information kit is free, for a phone call.

FLORAL GLASS MIRROR, INC.

895 Motor Parkway (800) 647-7672
Hauppauge NY 11788 (516) 234-2200

Floral provides beveled mirrors in all shapes and sizes, with ovals and circles in eleven sizes and three colors. Thicknesses up to 1".

FOLEY-BELSAW

6301 Equitable Rd.
Kansas City MO 64120

Write for information on their one-man sawmill and the free book *How to Saw Lumber*.

FOREDOM ELECTRIC CO.

16 Stony Hill Rd.
Bethel CT 06801 (203) 792-8622

Foredom's product manager asks that you call for their free catalog (and dealer's name) on Foredom flexible shaft tools including the "SR" reversible motor and 35,000 and 45,000 rpm Micro Motors. There is also a complete accessories catalog that covers tungsten carbide bits, ruby carvers, carbide burrs, and all sorts of cutting, grinding, and polishing accessories. Foredom is probably the oldest name in the flexible shaft tool industry, having started in 1922, and may well make the widest line of such tools today. I got confused and quit counting after noting fifteen different power heads!

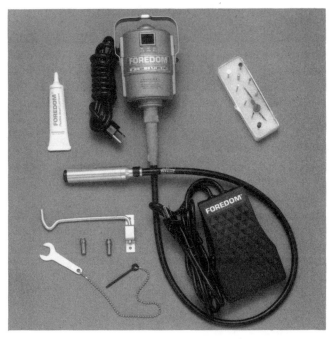

Foredom's 5240 power carving kit, with head, hand piece, foot switch, bits, and accessories.

Homer Formby behind his line of finishing and refinishing products.

Foredom's SR power head.

FORMBY'S WORKSHOP

Olive Branch MS 38654

Formby's finishes are designed for safety and ease of use. Formby's offers a full line, from finish removers and accessories (finish remover pads, steel wool pads, protective plastic covers, refinishing gloves, and more) to restoring finishes, wood stains, tung oils, and finish care products. The colorful and informative brochure is free for the asking.

Emma Samms refinishes a piece using Formby's refinisher.

FORREST MANUFACTURING COMPANY, INC.

461 River Rd.
Clifton NJ 07014   (800) 733-7111

A manufacturer of high grade saw blades, Forrest differentiates to the point where they offer different blade choices for table saws and radial arm saws. (The table saw blade is primarily a rip blade, though listed as all purpose. The radial

Formby's Wiping Stain, a gelled stain which is easy to apply.

arm saw blade, with sixty teeth, is virtually a cut-off blade.) As noted, Forrest products are top of the line, thus are somewhat pricey. I have seen their 80 tooth blade in action, however, after a long term of heavy use, and it still made some fine cuts. The woodworkers' catalog is free on request.

Forrest Woodworker II table saw blade.

FRANKLIN INTERNATIONAL

Consumer Products Division
2020 Bruck St.   (800) 877-4583
Columbus OH 43207   In OH: (614) 443-0241

The leading manufacturer of woodworking adhesives (and a leading maker of caulks and construction adhesives, some of which may be handy on some woodworking jobs). Franklin's Titebond and Titebond II are the most widely used woodworking adhesives in the United States. Titebond is a yellow aliphatic resin wood glue that is moderately moisture resistant. The much newer Titebond II is a waterproof glue that is the cheapest true waterproof woodworker's adhesive on the market. (On average, it is only about 15% more expensive than original Titebond. Comparisons might be made with epoxies and resorcinol for cost. Titebond II wins, though both epoxies and resorcinol offer other fea-

tures to help make up for great expense. TII cuts odor, complexity, and harmful vapor problems, as well as expense.) Check for the name of your nearest dealer.

FREUD

P.O. Box 7187
High Point NC 27264   (800) 472-7407

Jim Brewer at Freud supplied so much detailed information that, adding it to their three catalogs, I ended up spinning, trying to figure what to include and what to leave out. Their current new router bit catalog offers ninety-two pages of top grade bits. Call their 800 number for a copy of that catalog, their blade catalog, their hand tool catalog, or all three. Catalogs are free to readers of this book, so mention it. Some company detail, for those who have never heard of Freud (if any such woodworkers exist), must include the fact the company has been in business for over fifty years and has been in the U.S. market for upwards of twenty years. They use a special titanium-bonded carbide in their router bits, make their own carbide for greatest quality control, and provide special computer-controlled grinding to reduce vibration, burn, and chatter. I have used Freud bits and blades and a Freud router, and found they live up to company claims. Freud blades and bits are a bit pricey but durable and well made, which reduces problems with cost. Cost, figured realistically, is a result of price divided by value. And price can be reduced if you search through other catalogs offered in this book to find a good discount retailer.

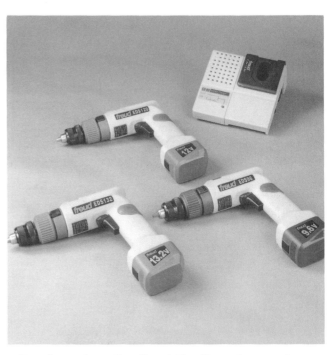

Freud's new line of cordless drills offers 9.6, 12, and 13.2 volt models to suit all purposes. They are truly finely made.

G & W TOOL CO., INC.

P.O. Box 691464
Tulsa OK 74169   (918) 486-2761

Free literature describes the Wagner Safe-T-Planer, an accessory that fits radial arm saws and drill presses. The planers are made of die cast aluminum and high speed steel that is precision ground. Basically, the tools turn a drill press or radial arm saw into a planer, allowing you to cut molding patterns, raised panels, tapered legs, rabbets, tenons, and similar patterns. The tool cannot kick back and is low cost. G & W Tool Co. sells directly, and the Wagner Safe-T-Planer is also available from most mail order houses.

G&W Wagner Safe-T-Planer in stages of assembly, with the sharpening stone on the right.

The Safe-T-Planer in use.

GENERAC CORPORATION

P.O. Box 8   (414) 544-4811
Waukesha WI 53187   FAX: (414) 544-4851

Generac Corporation makes a line of stand-alone generators meant primarily to supplement local power company transmissions during power failures, brownouts, and blackouts. The Generac models 3500 XL and 2500 XL are excellent units, and may also be used to provide job site power where no other power is available. (It seems unlikely, but one never really knows when such a unit might be handy. The two above are almost light enough [the heavier 3500 XL weighs only 110 pounds] to cart around easily.) The 3500 XL provides more than enough wattage to run a good-sized table saw (my figures show 25 amperes at 120 volts, with a surge allowance of about 6 more amps). It offers a 30 ampere 120 volt outlet (surge rated), or a 20 ampere 240 volt outlet, and its 190cc engine can run for about fifteen hours on its four gallon fuel load. Most major home center chains have one or both models, and there is a network of Generac distributors where you can get more information.

The Generac 3500XL lets you take the power to the work.

GENERAL TOOLS MFG. CO.

80 White St.
New York NY 10013   (212) 431-6499

A maker of small tools, General has a full line catalog. Call or write for information on the tool lines that include measuring tools, screwdrivers, and much more.

GIL-LIFT

1605 North River
Independence MO 64050   (816) 833-0611

For those of us who from time to time build wall-mounting cabinets, this lift for cabinet installation seems to be an ideal solution to a pernicious problem (getting the cabinet to stay in place without a helper and without a massive framework of aids, while attaching it to the wall). Gil Wyand makes only this one tool and will send free information on request.

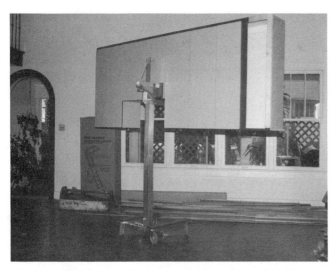

This Gil-Lift has a load on and demonstrates how it will save energy, time, and possible damage to your person and the materials.

The Gil-Lift moves cabinets into place and holds them there with no strain.

GILLIOM MANUFACTURING, INC.

P.O. Box 1018
St. Charles MO 63302   (314) 724-1812

If you have any desire to make your own power tools, kits from Gilliom may be the incentive you need to get started. The list includes a 12" bandsaw, an 18" bandsaw, a 10" tilt arbor table saw, a lathe and drill press combination, a 9" tilt-table table saw, a 6" belt sander, a spindle shaper, and a circular saw table, at $7.50 each or $25.00 for the package of eight plans. Gilliom also manufactures kits to help you in building the tools. The descriptive brochure is $2.00.

GOUGEON BROTHERS

100 Patterson Ave.
Bay City MI 48707   (517) 684-7286

The West System 1000 Polyurethane Varnish and epoxy adhesives are available from Gougeon Bros. Call or write for further information.

GRANBERG INTERNATIONAL

P.O. Box 425
Richmond CA 94807   (510) 237-2099

Granberg makes a chainsaw lumber mill that appears similar to one I used about twenty years ago. I believe the company thought it mailed more to me than it did (two photos and an empty envelope), but the mill is an attachment for your own chainsaw and is thus about the most economical kind of small sawmill you can find. The wide kerf chainsaw cut wastes more wood than do bandsaw and circular saw mills, and chainsaw mills are more time consuming to use, but the start-up cost is a small fraction of the cost of either of those types. Drop a line to the company to check out specifications and prices.

The Granberg chainsaw lumber mill, with a log that has been slabbed on one side.

The Granberg chainsaw mill handles many board widths easily.

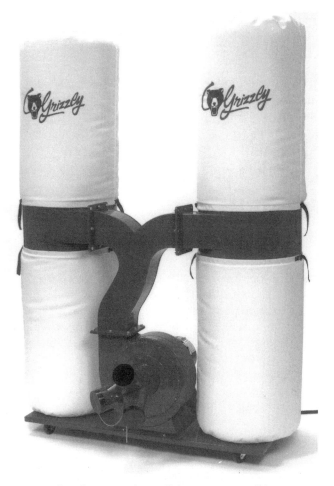

Grizzly's three port dust collector is a powerful unit.

GRIZZLY IMPORTS, INC.

West of Mississippi:
P.O. Box 2069
Bellingham WA 98227-2069   (800) 541-5537
East of the Mississippi:
2406 Reach Rd.
Williamsport PA 17701   (800) 523-4777

The Grizzly catalog, a sizable book (about 140 color pages) is free from either location, both of which are showroom and warehouse locations. Grizzly is a major importer of Taiwanese stationary tools but no longer stops there. Their catalog shows the expected lines of table saws, planers, dust collectors, sanders, jointers, bandsaws, and more. Added to that is Grizzly's line of accessories of many kinds, from sanding belts and abrasive discs to mortising attachments and chisels, plus their own line of framing and brad nailers and staplers. In addition, they carry Makita tools and Campbell-Hausfeld air compressors and accessories, plus a reasonable line of books and videos. Add to that a short but handy line of European cabinet hardware and more, and the catalog becomes very interesting.

This is Grizzly's heavy-duty planer on an HTC base (which Grizzly retails) for mobility around the shop.

HIRSH COMPANY

8051 Central Park   (800) 872-3279
Skokie IL 60076   (708) 673-6610

Hirsh makes various shelves and benches featuring at least
partial sheet metal construction. Call or write for more
information.

HITACHI

4487 Park Dr.   (800) 548-8259
Norcross GA 30093   (404) 925-1774
                              FAX: (404) 923-2117
7490 Lampson Ave.   (800) 548-8259
Garden Grove CA 92641   (714) 891-5330
                              FAX: (714) 898-9096

Hitachi tools have been in the U.S. market over a decade
now and have earned a reputation for quality. The line
consists of more than eighty-five tools for working wood,
concrete, metals, and other materials, with our emphasis
and interest riding on drills, including the cordless models;
circular saws, including miter saws up to 15" in blade
diameter; and a well-regarded slide-compound miter saw,
routers, planers, jointer-planers, a 12" table saw, and a 14½"
bandsaw. Hitachi will send along a mini-catalog on request.

Hitachi's belt sander removes lots of material quickly.

HORTON BRASSES

Nooks Hill Rd.
P.O. Box 120
Cromwell CT 06416   (203) 635-4400

Antique reproduction furniture hardware is featured in the
$3.00 catalog.

*The above photographs show a selection of hardware by
Horton Brasses.*

HTC PRODUCTS, INC.

120 E. Hudson
P.O. Box 839
Royal Oak MI 48608   (800) 624-2027

HTC is the top name in mobile bases for stationary power tools, with 200 standard models (a number that grows each year), and upwards of 1000 models in all. The new Brett Guards for table saws appear to be among the easiest to use protectors available. Most woodworkers I know have a pile of unused guards stuffed on back shelves. Even the industrial outfits and workers tend to pull them off, keeping them around for OSHA inspections and not using them otherwise. The reasons are simple: almost all guards are difficult to use, or to set up, often both. Difficulty in use makes for shortcuts that reduce guard effectiveness or make total removal the simplest option. Thus, if the Brett Guard does as claimed, acceptance will be phenomenal. The catalog is free, and your edition will be a new, full-color 16 pager.

HTC's outfeed table is up for use, and the Brett Saw Guard is in place.

The outfeed table and Brett Guard are ready for use. Note the mobile saw base.

Here, the HTC outfeed table is down to make space.

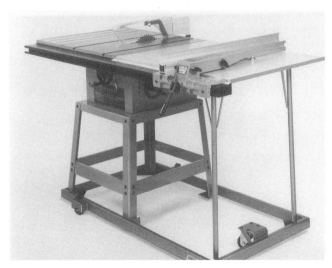

Another HTC mobile saw base.

HYDROCOTE

P.O. Box 160   (800) 229-4937
Tennent NJ 07763   (908) 257-4344

Hydrocote was one of the earliest companies manufacturing water-based clear finishes. Call or write for further information. I have used a number of the new water-based finishes, and may never go back to those thinned with mineral spirits. I have yet to try Hydrocote, but it does have a good reputation.

INDUSTRIAL ABRASIVES CO.

642 N. 8th St.   (800) 428-2222
Reading PA 19612   In PA: (800) 222-2292

Sanding belts and other abrasive tools are featured in this manufacturer's free catalog. Buy a dozen sanding belts and get a dozen free.

INJECTA MACHINERY

2217 El Sol Ave.
Altadena CA 91001   (818) 797-8262

Call or write for free information on Inca power tools.

IRWIN COMPANY

Wilmington OH 45177   (800) 338-2158

Irwin manufactures a full line of popularly priced carbide-tipped saw blades, plus top quality lines, plus drill and router bits in many configurations. Write for information.

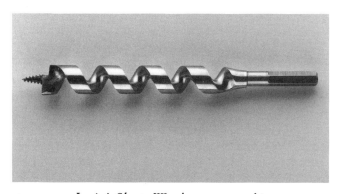

Irwin's Shorty Woodmaster auger bit.

J.A. HARCHUCK SALES

1649 Beighley Rd.
Apollo PA 15613   (412) 733-7555

John Harchuck is the national sales representative for Croix Air Products, makers of high-volume, low-pressure spray finish equipment. The Croix line is American made, and the company is the oldest in manufacturing this type of spray finishing equipment. This is not a low cost setup, but the small CX-5 might do well for moderate cost. Write or call for free brochures and price lists.

Croix CX-12 HVLP (high volume, low pressure) spray equipment. Courtesy of J.A. Harchuck Sales.

HARDEL MUTUAL PLYWOOD CORPORATION

P.O. Box 3265   (206) 754-6030
Olympia WA 98507   FAX: (206) 943-9352

Hardel is a producer of plywood, located in an area where many such producers congregate. The Hardel plywood lines includes sanded plywoods, 303 plywood sidings, and marine grade panels. They also produce 9' x 10' structural sheathing panels. Sanded precision dimension panels are available from ¼" to 1½" thick and in panel sizes 4x8, 4x9, 4x10, 5x8, 5x9, 5x10. Write or call for a free brochure.

HARTCO QUALITY WOOD FLOORING

900 S. Gay St.
Suite 1902
Knoxville TN 37902   (615) 544-0767

Finished flooring may be handy for a number of project uses, including tops and insets where proper finishing might otherwise be difficult. Also, you can use parquet and other patterns far more easily than you can cut the materials yourself, with edging readily available in the same wood and finish you have selected for the main pattern. Drop a note for the free catalog and list of distributors.

JDS COMPANY

800 Dutch Square Blvd.
Suite 200 (800) 382-2637
Columbia SC 29210 (803) 798-1600

The Accu-Miter free brochure presents a look at an intriguing tool. The Accu-Miter is a replacement miter gauge, with a precision protractor scale, a rigid front fence with a telescopic extension (two sizes, one to 18½" in length; the larger to 24½") and some related accessories and custom parts. It's durable, of die-cast construction, and offers a stop that may be inserted in either end, for accurate multiple cuts. JDS also makes the Multi-Router machine, which offers quick setup and efficient cutting of many joints, from mortise and tenon on through varieties of dovetail, compound angle tenons, round tenons, and more.

JET EQUIPMENT & TOOLS

P.O. Box 1477
1901 Jefferson Ave. (206) 572-5000
Tacoma WA 98401-1477 FAX: (206) 383-8705

Jet imports a full line of stationary and other power tools, many of which are of interest to both the hobby woodworker and the professional. Table saws run up to 16" in blade diameter (from 10"), and there are lathes, planers, jointers, drill presses, bandsaws, scroll saws, pneumatic tools (including various nailers and staplers), and air compressors. There are a good number of sanders, shapers, and dust collectors. Jet has a large number of dealers, and will supply information on different tools if you give them a call. As noted, the range is wide. In planers alone, Jet offers a 12" lightweight; a 15" heavy duty; four 20" (often with larger planers, the major difference is in the power of the motors used, with

This is Jet's JWL01236 wood lathe.

lighter duty models using single phase 230 volt, and heavy-duty bombers needing three phase 230 or 460 volt), and a 24" planer (this uses three phase, period, with a 10 horse main motor, a 1 horse feed roller motor, and a ½ horse power table motor).

JIFFY FOAM, INC.

221 Third St. (800) 344-8997
Newport RI 02830 (401) 846-7870
(401) 847-9966

Jiffy Foam manufactures Balsa Foam, a paintable, carvable foam that works nicely for many carving demands and can even be cut with cookie cutters. It's great as a starter for wood carvers, and can be sawed, carved, and chiseled, will take impressions, sands well without gum-up, and takes oil-base paints. It glues readily with polyvinyl resin (white) glues. Generally available at hobby shops, Balsa Foam can also be located if you call Don Anderson at the above numbers. (Jiffy Foam is *not* a retailer, but will set up a small trial order for a hobby or similar shop.) Jiffy Foam sent me a couple of samples and, though I'm not a wood carver, I was impressed with the strength and actual ease of carving with a sharp tool but resistance with a dull tool, so press-in impressions work nicely. The material is a dun color, and does not resemble Styrofoam at all — it's much finer grained.

KASCO

Rural Route 3
Box 393
Shelbyville IN 46176

Write for information on the Kasco Portable Band Saw Mill. Such sawmills tend to be more costly than chainsaw driven mills, but also tend to waste far less wood.

KELLER & COMPANY

1327 I St.
Petaluma CA 94952 (707) 763-9336

The Keller dovetail system consists of three different size dovetail template sets. It differs from most others in its price range in being non-adjustable. While the lack of adjustability would seems to be a feature that detracts from the system, it actually allows very rapid setup and quick production of dovetails, reducing overall problems that on other systems may come close to driving you back to handcut dovetails (almost). Each Keller dovetail set (models 1601, 2401, 3601) has two templates (one for the dovetails and one for the pins), two carbide-tipped router bits (one dovetail and one straight), and a really simple and good instruction manual. You add only supports for the templates, after which the units are clamped onto the pieces to be cut, the cuts are made, and your project is assembled. It takes about ten minutes to finish detailed template setup after mounting. I have set up and used two of the Keller sets, and find them, as advertised, easy to use and of fine quality. If you want to machine cut dovetails and nothing else, then the Keller sets are for you. Give Dave a call if you have any questions on availability, price, or if you want a brochure or the new video (currently $8.95 plus $2.00 shipping).

Here is one part of the Keller template set in use to produce dovetails.

KIMBALL SIGN COMPANY

2602 Whitaker St.
Savannah GA 31401   (912) 232-6561

Ken Kimball's K55 and K66 Woodcarvers are described in a $2.00 full-color brochure, which includes short instruction on how difficult the setup is to use, as well as a look at what each model provides. The K55 is the larger unit, and both kits may be had ranging from basic units to fully equipped setups, including routers and dust collection systems.

KITKRAFT

Box 2145
Trinity TX 75862

If you're interested in dulcimer kits, write for Kitkraft's free brochure.

KLEIN DESIGN INC.

17910 SE 110th St.
Renton WA 98059   (206) 226-5937

Klein Design produces two miniature lathes, one of which is a full pattern lathe with a 12" bed length. The other is a

short bed model. In addition, many jigs and tools are available for the lathes (threading jigs, scroll chuck, custom jaws, indexing system, hole-drilling guides, and more). Videos on lathe use are also sold, with a series of five covering just about everything you wish to know about miniature turning, from using unusual materials — horn, bone, cast polyester, mother of pearl, Corian, and others — to making turned boxes with threaded lids. Call or drop a note for the latest brochure and price lists.

Klein Design's standard wood lathe.

KLINGSPOR ABRASIVES

P.O. Box 2367   (800) 645-5555
Hickory NC 28603   (704) 322-3030

Klingspor is an abrasives manufacturer that also sells its products by mail, which makes them ideal for inclusion in this book. Send or call for a free color catalog, which will vary in size and content according to sales, and similar requirements. Headquartered in Hickory, NC, Klingspor has recently expanded to Ventura, CA, to better serve that market. Products include belt and disc abrasives with a wide variety of coat styles (open and closed) added to different backing materials. Prices are reasonable to low, with quantity discounts.

KLOCKIT

P.O. Box 636
Lake Geneva WI 53147   (800) KLOCKIT

Distributes clock kits, movements, faces, and virtually all clock-making accessories. The Klockit emphasis is on quartz battery movements, including some moderately massive chiming pendulum and dual pendulum types (not as long or large as truly massive mechanical movements, with a maximum bob diameter of about 3½" on a 20" long pendulum). You will also find mechanicals, with cable-driven movements, bobs over 10" in diameter, and a wide variety of grandfather and grandmother clock faces. Case kits, full kits, cuckoo clocks, fretwork project kits (available ready to cut or already laser cut), and music box kits with fifty-note movements. There is even a two-page spread of wristwatches and a fair assortment of accessories such as brad point drill bits, sanding drums, Forstner bits, and wood and brass parts. Catalog is free.

KUEMPEL CHIME

21195 Minnetonka Blvd.
Excelsior MN 55331

Red-I-Cut clock kits and movements are listed in the free Kuempel catalog.

LAGUNA TOOLS

2081 Laguna Canyon Rd.   (800) 234-1976
Laguna Beach CA 92651   (714) 494-7006

Call or write for free details on the Robland X31 one-man shop, an 1100 pound multi-tool shop that uses three 3 horse motors to power a 12" jointer/planer, a 10" table saw with a 50" sliding table, and a shaper-mortiser. Cast iron construction gives accuracy and durability.

LAMPI

7272 Governors Dr. West
P.O. Box 1769   (205) 830-3110
Huntsville AL 35807   FAX: (205) 830-9518

Lampi makes various lamps useful on projects or around a shop. Most are of the types useful when enclosed in a shelf or cabinet project, or placed nearby. The lamps are available in single quantities at many do-it-yourself centers, but for special orders, you may get in touch with Lampi directly.

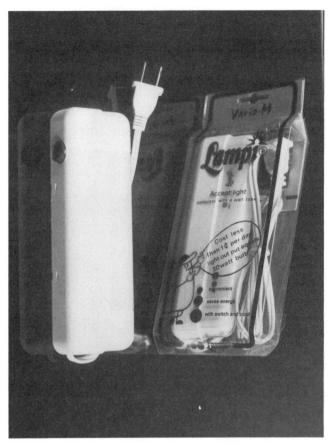

Lampi's Vario-M light is for use in china cabinets and similar places.

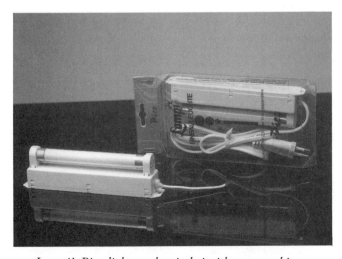

Lampi's Pico light works nicely inside stereo cabinets.

LASER MACHINING, INC.

500 Laser Dr.   (715) 247-3285
Somerset WI 54025   FAX: (715) 247-5650

Call or write for information on laser cutting equipment.

LEIGH INDUSTRIES, LTD.

P.O. Box 357
1585 Broadway St.   (800) 663-8932
Port Coquitlam BC   (604) 464-2700
Canada V3C 4K6   FAX: (604) 464-7404

Leigh jigs offer an incredible variety of choices in joint-making, starting with dovetails. The basic jig gives the ability to cut almost every kind of dovetail, including through, half-blind, sliding, end-on-end, and more, in wood to 1¼" thick. A multiple mortise and tenon attachment and a vast array of cutters further assist you in doing what you wish to do. The catalog is free, and beautifully done, and Leigh sells directly, as well as through distributors.

LEINBACH MACHINERY

5000 Reynolda Rd.
Winston-Salem NC 27106   (919) 924-4115

Write or call for information on the Kasco air helmet line (made in Italy).

LENEAVE MACHINERY & SUPPLY COMPANY

305 West Morehead St.   (800) 442-2302
Charlotte NC 28202   (704) 376-7421

Call or write for information on Northstate stationary power tools. Most of these are truly heavy-duty units, but some may be of interest to hobby woodworkers.

LIE-NIELSEN TOOLWORKS

Route 1
Warren ME 04684   (800) 327-2520

These makers of heirloom quality hand tools offer a free brochure. The tools are lovely, lovingly made, and should be used the same way.

LIGNOMAT USA LTD.

P.O. Box 30145   (800) 227-2105
Portland OR 92301   (503) 257-8957

Lignomat moisture meters are probably the best known of all such units. A free brochure explains one or more of the many models they produce, with an array starting at the pocket-sized (if you have a good-sized free pocket: this is the one I use, and I keep it clipped to my belt) Mini-Lignometer, the Lignomaster K100, and the G1000. There is an in-kiln model too, and a newly introduced Thermo-hygrometer for shops and other wood storage areas. The Thermo-hygrometer may be hand-held, wall mounted, or set on any convenient flat surface such as a desk. For the person who has everything, including a drying kiln, Lignomat produces a computerized kiln control system as well.

Lignomat's Thermo-Hygrometer.

I'm currently using a Mini-Ligno such as this and find it handy and accurate enough for general woodworking shop uses.

LOBO POWER TOOLS

9034 Bermudez St.   (213) 949-3747
Pico Rivera CA 90660   Order line: (800) 786-5626
          Atlanta: (404) 416-6006

Lobo imports stationary power tools, including table saws, bandsaws, spindle shapers, jointers, and wide belt sanders. They offer a free brochure and a $3.00 catalog, and sell direct.

LOCTITE CORP.

4450 Cranwood Court   (800) 321-9188
Cleveland OH 44128   (216) 475-3600

You may wonder what Loctite Corporation is doing in a book for woodworkers. For one thing, their Fast Orange hand cleaner is one of the best on the market and clears stain, lacquer, paint, glue, and almost all imaginable glop from the hands and arms. Next up, Loctite's namesake, the various thread lockers, are very helpful around any shop, when assembling and reassembling and adjusting tools. Add in a variety of belt dressings (try some on your table saw and other belt drives and note the reduction in noise, and seeming increase in power — from increased grip and general efficiency, plus added belt life), silicone sealers, epoxies, and some other products, and you will find many reasons for considering Loctite products. They have recently come out with a new packaging method for epoxies, in both five-minute and ninety-minute set versions. No measuring, no mixing tools, no mess. The ninety-minute set is handy for a number of woodworking purposes, and the quick grab will do for some repairs. Most information is available at your dealer, but if you can't locate a dealer, or want details the dealer doesn't have, give them a call.

This model's hands are only art-director dirty, but Fast Orange works for really grimy, paint-gummed hands too. Courtesy of Loctite Corp.

LOUISIANA-PACIFIC CORPORATION

111 S.W. Fifth Ave.
Portland OR 97204

Louisiana-Pacific produces almost all kinds of plywood and other wood products, both as engineered wood products (plywoods, oriented strand boards, and waferboards, among others) and as lumber, including redwood and pressure-treated versions. Drop them a note for a brochure and the name of a local dealer or distributor.

LRH ENTERPRISES, INC.

CO-ST Cutter Bits

7101 Valjean Ave.	(800) 423-2544
Van Nuys CA 91406	(818) 782-0226

Shaper cutters from LRH in stock patterns appear to cover about any profile one is apt to want, and the company also does custom cutter production. The newest line is the CO-ST Cutters designed to fit ½" and ¾" spindle shapers (sizes more likely to be in the small shop than the larger units). Give them a call to request literature or information.

LRH CO-ST Cutter bits.

LRH CO-ST bits.

MAFELL NORTH AMERICA

80 Earheart Dr.
Unit 9
Williamsville NY 14221

(716) 626-9303
(716) 626-9304

Mafell North America imports German tools that are best described as unusual. Many are designed for timber framing use, including a two-man circular saw with a 25³⁄₁₆" blade. Their small circular saw takes blades 13¾" to 17¾" and offers cuts to 5³⁄₁₆" deep at a 45 degree angle! The little saw weighs 63 pounds, versus 116.6 pounds for its big brother. In addition, Mafell imports the Erika push-pull table saw that provides the benefits of both table and radial arm saws in one unit, with free blade operation allowing 11" of blade travel through the wood, and with a fixed blade operation similar to other ⅝" arbor, 10" to 12" blade diameter saws (the Erika takes an 11" blade, something of an oddity in this country). The Erika is super light at 82 pounds and takes a wide assortment of accessories and supports, including a sliding table, micro adjust rip fence attachment, and double cross and miter cut fence guide. Tools are pricey, as European woodworking tools tend to be, but offer features not found in U.S.-made units. Also offered are a shaper, a planer-thicknesser-jointer, a dust and chip collector, a plunge cut router, an orbital sander, a belt sander, a jig saw, and many timber framing tools such as chainsaw mortisers. Call or write for information. Erika stationary tools catalog $1.00.

MAKITA U.S.A., INC.

14930 Northam St.
La Mirada CA 90638

(714) 522-8088

Makita has recently added 12 volt cordless driver/drills, impact drivers, and hammer-drills to their line of cordless tools. This brings the Makita line of cordless power tools in line with other makers who had set 12 volt as the standard for top-of-the-line models. Also new from Makita is a cordless stapler that drives as many as 750 ⅞" long staplers on a single charge. A random orbit sander helps round out their line of woodworking sanders, so Makita now has a very wide line of power tools, from the cordless to corded drills, circular saws, miter and compound miter saws (I've been using a Makita 10" compound miter saw for some time and find it remarkably good), generators, portable planers, electric chainsaws, a 14" bandsaw, a dust collector, a 12" portable planer, a planer-jointer, a couple of table saws, routers, and much more. Call or write for dealer's name.

Makita's 12 volt cordless drill has a nice shape.

Makita's entry in the random orbit sander race.

MASON & SULLIVAN

586 Higgins Crowell Rd.
W. Yarmouth
Cape Cod MA 02673

The Mason & Sullivan line includes antique reproduction clock kits and parts. The catalog is free. Woodcraft now owns Mason & Sullivan.

MASTODON TOOL

P.O. Box 17506
Portland OR 97217   (503) 283-6838

Jaw extenders fit standard ¾" pipe clamps and give an 8" deep reach, with swivel ends. Give a call or drop a note for further details.

MESA VISTA DESIGN

804 Tulip Rd.
Rio Rancho NM 87124   (505) 892-0293

Write or call for information on the Grip-Tite magnetic featherboard.

METABO CORP.

P.O. Box 2287
1231 Wilson Dr.   (215) 436-5900
West Chester PA 19380   FAX: (215) 436-9072

Metabo is one of the world's leading makers of power tools and abrasives, with production facilities in both Nurtingen, Germany, and the U.S. Hand power tools are the products of most immediate interest to woodworkers, and the line is extensive, including a number of cordless drills, up to and including a superb 12 volt model, a circular saw, reciprocating saw, corded drills, and other tools. The catalog is free on request.

Metabo's random orbit sander.

Metabo's jig saw.

MICRO-MARK

340-1077 Snyder Ave.   (800) 225-1066
Berkley Heights NJ 07922   (908) 464-6764

Write or call for information on the tiny Miter Rite small scale (54 tpi saw) miter box.

MICRO-SURFACE FINISHING PRODUCTS

P.O. Box 818   (800) 225-3006
Wilton IA 52778   (319) 732-3240
            FAX: (319) 732-3390

Micro-Surface will send free information on its micro-mesh abrasives. I got a quick demonstration and find them remarkable, within the limits for which they are intended. If you want to produce a truly slick, high gloss finish, there may be nothing better. If you are polishing out old or new finishes, shining plastics or metals in the course of projects, give these a try. There are kits to restore plastic, a paint and plastic maintenance kit, and a metal finishing kit. Specialized kits include those for high luster paint finishes, hobby and models, woodworking, boats, households. Micro-mesh regular is available in 1500, 1800, 2400, 3200, 3600, 4000, 6000, 8000, and 12000 grades, in 6x12 and 12x12 sheets, and 4" x 50' and other roll sizes. Coarser grades, Micro-mesh MX, are available, in 100, 150, 180, 240 (after this, you're into finish polishing applications for wood; infrequently, you may wish a 320 grit for working bare wood, but not often), 320, 360, 400, 600, 800, and 1200, in the same sheet and roll sizes, plus ⅝" to 2" wide tapes. Call the 800 number for your closest distributor.

MILWAUKEE ELECTRIC TOOL CORP.

13135 W. Lisbon Rd.   (414) 781-3600
Brookfield WI 53005   (414) 781-3611
Milwaukee Electric Tool (Canada) Ltd.
755 Progress Ave.
Scarborough ONT   (416) 439-4181
Canada M1H 2W7   FAX: (416) 439-6210

Milwaukee has long been one of the leading wide line electric tool manufacturers in the hemisphere, to the point that at least one of their tools' names, the Sawzall, has almost become a generic term (in this case, for a reciprocating saw). Ask a plumber or remodeling contractor about a recip saw, and the saw will almost certainly be called the "sawsall." A recent addition to the line is the 10", 15 ampere Magnum miter saw, and the line goes on through a multitude of the usual top quality tools, including routers, drills, driver-drills, cordless driver drills, circular saws, grinders, sanders and polishers, plus new random orbit sanders, heat guns, and a multitude of accessories. The catalog is free.

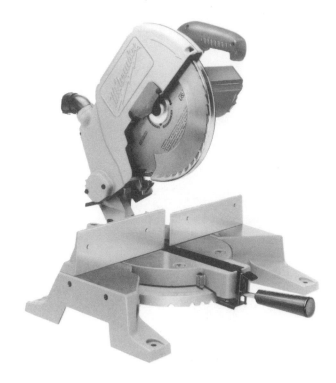

Milwaukee Magnum miter saw.

Milwaukee screw shooter kit.

MINUTEMAN

115 N. Monroe St.
P.O. Box 8
Waterloo WI 53594   (800) 733-1776
            (414) 478-2001

Call or write for details on Minuteman's Mini-Flo Furniture Stripping System.

MINWAX COMPANY INC.

15 Mercedes Dr.
Montvale NJ 07645

Probably every non-novice woodworker is familiar with the name Minwax. I sure remember them from some time ago,

and find their products stand up to and improve with time. Minwax now offers their version of the new lines of water-based polys, called Polycrylic. Polycrylic offers water cleanup, low odor, fast drying (thirty minutes dry to the touch), non-

Minwax Polyshade going on.

Minwax Polyshade project when finished.

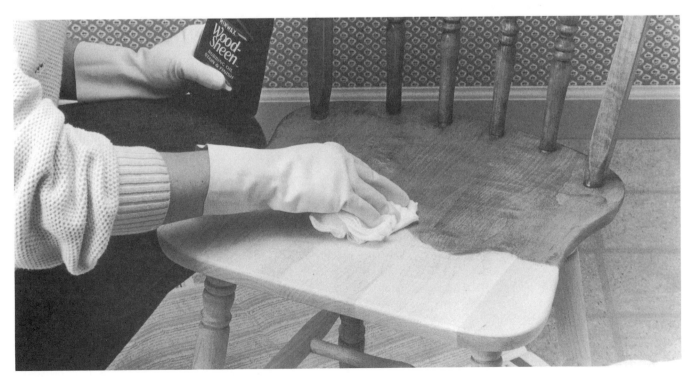

Minwax Woodsheen gives a hand-rubbed look with very little effort.

flammability, and the non-yellowing look that is almost universal among these finishes. (So far, I have used four, all excellent and all non-yellowing, leaving wood with a more natural look after finishing.) Minwax also offers WoodSheen Frosted Stain & Finish, a one-step pastel penetrating oil finish that is really great if you like pastel look finishes. Depending on application, it can be a pickled or more solid color look. WoodSheen also comes in a rubbing oil stain look that just wipes on in seven stains. Of course, Minwax still offers its standard line of stains, polyurethane, tung oil, and antique finishes, plus Polyshades, a combined stain and polyurethane finish in one. Minwax's Pastels stains round out the lines, but there is also the Watco line of Danish Oil finishes. Write and ask for brochures on any of these products.

MLCS, LTD.

P.O. Box 4053 C13   (800) 533-9298
Rydal PA 19046   FAX: (215) 938-5070

The free MLCS catalog features router bits, but also offers a few other items. The router bits are reputed to be top quality (I have never used this brand) and come in a wide variety of profiles, including raised panel, stile and rail, multiform molding makers, French provincial, double ogee and double flute raised panel bits, an ogee raised panel bit with an undercutter, crown molding bits, and a slew of other molding bits, plus standard cove and bead, chamfer, Roman ogee, round over, beading, drawer and finger pull, ogee fillet, and thumbnail bits. There are round nose bits, core box bits, keyhole cutting bits, dish cutters, spiral downcut bits, door lip bits, hinge mortising bits, straight bits, bottom cleaning bits, lock miter bits, finger joint bits, tongue and groove bits, flush trimming bits, and others. Other products include Forstner drill bits, from ¼" to 3⅛", shaper cutters, their own router table, an adjustable corner clamp, and other items. The catalog is definitely worth looking at, the inventory is large, and there are experienced woodworkers on staff to help with questions.

MR. MAC'S PRODUCTS

11 Creek Ridge Rd.
Greensboro NC 27406   (800) 333-3262

Call or write for details on Mr. Mac's Wood Fix rebuilder.

MULE CABINETMAKER MACHINE, INC.

519 Mill St.
P.O. Box 731   (800) 563-MULE
Lockport NY 14095   (416) 727-7090

I had one of the early production model Mule sliding tables and loved it. The newer ones appear to be less prone to minor problems and offer more capacities. Write or call for information.

NELSON & JACOBSON, INC.

3546 N. Clark St.
Chicago IL 60657

Nelson & Jacobson makes and sells the Electro bandsaw brazer, a tool that may seem totally beyond the needs of hobby woodworkers but is nearly essential to anyone who depends on a bandsaw for major parts of their woodworking. This inexpensive (currently $89.75, F.O.B. factory) brazer allows quick making of new blades from coil bandsaw stock and rapid repair of broken blades. Operation is simple and quick and is easy enough to allow use of the bandsaw for internal sawing, which requires breaking and rebrazing the bandsaw blade.

NEOTERIK HEALTH TECHNOLOGIES, INC.

401 Main St.
Woodsboro MD 21798   (301) 845-2777

Call or write for informaiton on the Mini-Breezer air helmet.

NORTH BAY FORGE

Box S
Waldron WA 98297

As with all hand-forged tools, North Bay's products tend to be pricey as compared to factory-made items. In many senses, it's a matter of choice when selecting tools, though a handmade tool has a greater beauty (and I don't think good machine-made tools are ugly at all, though cheaply made ones sure are) that is often worth the cost. With some makers, the beauty extends into the tool's handling. I can't comment on North Bay's tool handling, but the production is definitely by hand and in the old manner. North Bay Forge is located on Waldron Island, which has no phones (note the lack of phone number above) and lacks electricity! That doesn't mean no machines are used to produce North Bay Forge tools, but it does mean greater attention must be paid to each operation. The catalog, featuring scorps, drawknives, and carver's knives, is free.

NORTHWOOD INDUSTRIAL MACHINERY

11534 Commonwealth Dr.   (502) 267-5504
Louisville KY 40299   FAX: (502) 267-2332

Write or call for catalog on planers and dust collectors.

NORTON

Consumer Marketing
1 Bond St.
Worcester MA 01606   (508) 795-5000

I'm not sure of Norton's exact placement in the list of abrasives manufacturers, except that it has to be close to the top in size and in quality. There are abrasives for almost every purpose one might imagine, and a huge number of them are useful for woodworking chores. I have just received an interesting brochure covering woodworking sanding products that will allow you to choose and specify, to your dealer, the Norton products you need. The brochure is beautifully done and is available from the Abrasives Marketing Group, at the address above.

NOVA TOOL CO.

12500 Finnegan Rd.
P.O. Box 29341   Except NE: (800) 826-7606
Lincoln NE 68529   (402) 464-0511

Many woodworkers like to use a branding iron to let people know just who made a particularly fine piece. The Nova version is solid brass, and costs $26.00 (plus $3.00 shipping and handling), or you may call or write for the free brochure.

NYLE CORPORATION

P.O. Box 1107   (800) 777-NYLE
Bangor ME 04401   (207) 989-4335

Nyle lumber-drying kilns are available in many sizes. Call for further information.

OLDHAM-UNITED STATES SAW

Burt NY 14028   (716) 778-8588
                       (800) 828-9000

The Oldham-United States Saw catalog of saw blades, router bits, and abrasive wheels provides some major choices, from ultra-thin kerf carbide blades (Roadrunner series), to carbide tooth nail-cutting blades, steel saw blades, Wizard and Supreme Wizard premium series. (The Wizard series is designed for power mitering, and comes in appropriate sizes from 8¼" to 15"; the Supreme Wizard series is for table and radial arm saws. Both series are cut-off styles with 60 or 80 teeth.) You will also find three styles of dado blade, plus masonry and metal-cutting abrasive wheels, and Viper router bits. A comprehensive array. Literature is free.

P-Z DESIGN SPECIALITIES

10429 Campana Dr.
Sun City AZ 85381   (602) 972-3607

If you draw your own plans, call or write for more information on the Sit-N-Stand portable studio drafting setup.

PAINT STROKES

Civic Center Dr.
N. Las Vegas NV 89030   (800) 468-3779

Paint Strokes offers the Original Old World Crackle Refinishing Kit in three colors, for use on picture frames, chairs, tables, boxes, lamps, and other items. The finish is simple, in three steps (about two less than required for clear finishing an oak desk I'm currently building), non-toxic (I wish my desk finish job were — the paste filler smells nasty), non-flammable (no comment), and cleans up with water (the final coats do). Get information by writing or calling.

PARKS CORPORATION

P.O. Box 5   (800) 225-8543
Somerset MA 02726   (508) 679-5938
                          FAX: (508) 674-8404

Carver Tripp water-based finishes from Parks cover a wide range of finishing needs. Because they are water-based, solvent vapors are not a problem, meaning there is less chance of atmospheric poisoning and reduced chance of explosion or fire. Water-based finishes are always the wintertime choice unless the shop has extensive ventilation equipment. Carver Tripp's lines cover polyurethanes, stains, Danish finish (combines pigments and resins for a one-step wipe-on finish), sanding sealer, and high gloss polyurethane enamels. Pastel tint bases are also available. Drop them a note or give a call for literature on any of the Carver Tripp products.

Carver Tripp water-based finishes, from Parks Corp.

This is Carver Tripp Danish finish, which is also water-based for safe application and easy cleanup.

Penn State's stationary belt-disc sander.

PECO SALES, INC.

P.O. Box 8122   (800) 346-6939
Jackson MS 39284   FAX: (601) 355-5126

The Protimeter wood moisture meter from Peco Sales is a wide range unit (6% to 60%, instead of the more usual 6% to 20 or 30%). Price is said to be low. Call for more information and the name of a local dealer.

PENN STATE INDUSTRIES

2850 Comly Rd.   (800) 288-7297
Philadelphia PA 19154   (215) 676-7609

Penn State Industries presents a catalog of hobby woodworking machines in low to moderate price range. Three dust collector sizes are available, including a portable model with a 760 cubic foot per minute capacity. Other machines, including a 12" portable planer, a 6" x 48" belt sander with 9" disc, a three wheel bandsaw, a wood lathe, and a pile of other tools and accessories that make the dust to be collected. The catalog is free, and interesting.

Penn State's Super 125 (12.5") portable planer.

PERFORMANCE COATINGS, INC.

P.O. Box 1569 (800) 468-8820
Ukiah CA 95482 In CA: (800) 468-8817

Call or write for information on penetrating oil finishes, including Penofin.

PERFORMAX PRODUCTS, INC.

1211 Woodlake Dr. (800) 334-4910
Burnsville MN 55337 (616) 895-9922

If you do much wide board glue-up, the Performax drum sander setup for radial arm saws may be of great interest and help. Because of the one-side-open design, you can sand panels to 44" wide. Call or write for brochures and the name of your nearest dealer.

PHANTOM ENGINEERING, INC.

1122 S. State St.
Suite 21 (800) 279-4570
Provo UT 84606 (801) 377-5757

The Woodchuck indexing system works with your router to produce fancy beading, twisted beading, fluting, and all sorts of other shapes, starting with a rough piece of stock, milling on one to thirty-six surfaces. Free information, or send $2.00 for information and a copy of *The Phantom Woodworker*.

PLASTI-KOTE

P.O. Box 708 (800) 431-5928
Medina OH 44258 (216) 725-4511

The Authographics pen applies lines of gold and silver, while the Plasti-Kote line of aerosol paints has a noted reputation. Call or write for further information.

POOTATUCK CORP.

P.O. Box 24
Windsor VT 05089 (802) 674-5984

The maker of the Lion miter trimmer will send a free brochure on request. This guillotine-style miter trimmer is exceptionally accurate and relatively low cost. The tool uses razor sharp knives to do the trimming, leaving a very smooth cut. Pootatuck sells by mail order, as well as serving as manufacturer and distributor.

Pootatuck's Lion Miter trimmer uses guillotine blades instead of a saw.

PORTA-NAILS, INC.

P.O. Box 1257 (800) 634-9281
Wilmington NC 28402 (919) 762-6334

Porta-Nails has a family of woodworking machines that differ in kind from many other tool families. The PNI family revolves around routers but only partially around traditional routers. Their panel template and router arc attachment use

PNIs Ring Master.

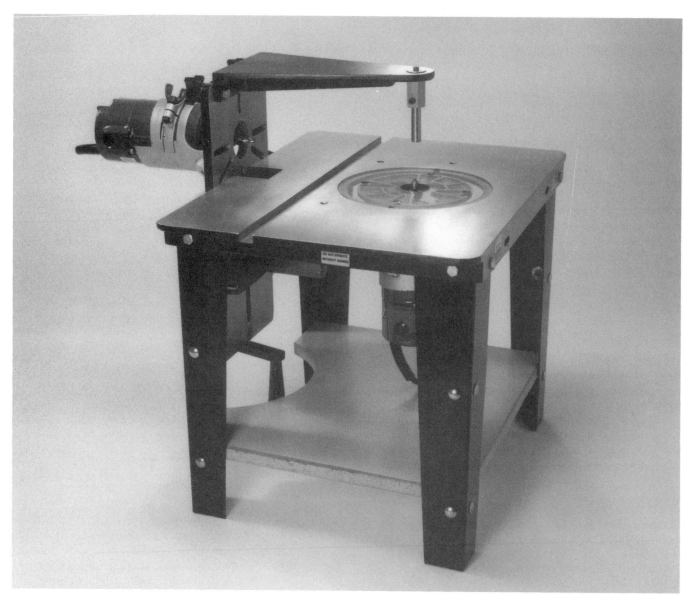

PNIs Router Mate.

standard routers and are described in a free brochure that goes on to describe the Router Mate, which converts a standard router to an overarm precision router; the Ring Master, which cuts rings from wood; and the Dowel Mate, which first clamps the wood then shoots in two dowel holes. A second product sheet describes the Universal Router Table, which sets up as a router table, joint maker, or pin router, using the same unit and two router motors.

PORTER-CABLE

P.O. Box 2468
Jackson TN 38302   (901) 668-8600

Porter-Cable is one of the smaller of the major United States tool manufacturers, but manufactures a wide line of portable power tools with quality second to none. Circular saws, a 10" power miter-saw, routers (up to 3¼ horsepower five speed monsters, both fixed and plunge, that operate and endure with any routers on the market from anyone), router bits, bayonet saws, the quietest of all biscuit joiners, sanders (belt, orbital, random orbit, and circular), plus drills in a line that includes several models of the famed Magnaquench cordless, which was one of the first of the 12 volt cordless drills and remains one of the most powerful. The Porter-Cable tool line goes on through portable bandsaws, recipro-

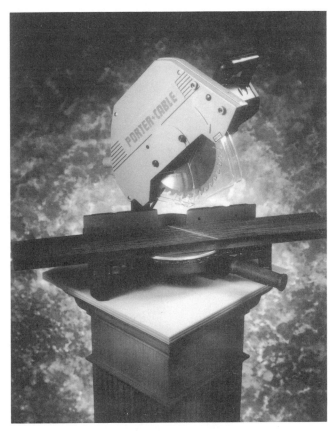

Porter-Cable's biscuit jointer is the quietest made.

Porter-Cable's 10" miter saw offers a laser-guided cut line.

Porter-Cable's new 24" Omni-Jig produces sliding dovetail, half-blind, through, and other dovetails, plus box joints.

cating saws, shears, grinders, polishers, and more. Write for a copy of their free catalog if your interest in hand-held power tools extends to industrial-quality tools into, and beyond, the above range.

POWERMATIC

McMinnville TN 37110   (800) 248-0144
(615) 473-5551

Powermatic is one of the big three (my classification) in woodworking power tools. It offers top quality for a good price, plus a wide range of tools and power supplies. Table saws, scroll saws, planers, lathes, jointers, shapers, belt and disc sanders, drill presses, bandsaws, grinders, and others. In recent years, Powermatic has come out with its Artisan series meant for contractors, small shops, and hobbyists. These are

lower powered, lower cost machines that still retain the Powermatic aura. The 6" Artisan jointer, at 198 pounds, has only its basic purpose in common with the 1350 pound 17" jointer and its 108" long table. Their catalog is free and truly worth looking at.

Powermatic's Artisan 10" table saw is designed for upper end hobby and light shop woodworking use.

PROCORP INC.

P.O. Box 5218
Grove City FL 34295   (813) 698-0222

Procorp manufactures flexible shaft rotary power tools offering state-of-the-art equipment under the Mastercarver name. The system includes a ¼ horse, reversible 19,000 rpm motor, a 38½" flexible shaft, and a reciprocating handpiece with five cutting blades.

RAINBOW WOODS

20 Andrews St.   (800) 423-2762
Newnan GA 30263   FAX: (404) 251-2761

Rainbow Woods offers hardwood turnings. You will find, in the free Rainbow Woods catalog, jewelry shapes, jewelry findings ("hardware" to other woodworkers), hardwood dowels, dowel caps, wheels in many sizes, axle pegs, smokestacks, all-purpose and tie rack pegs, barrels listed as cargo, along with oil drums and milk cans, blocks from ½" to 1½" square, peg people, round balls to 3" diameter, candle cups, Shaker and mug pegs, furniture plugs and buttons, dowel pins, fruits and vegetables, spools, pull knobs, gallery rail spindles, larger birch spindles, salt and pepper sets, and more. There may not be every turned wood part available, but there are plenty for most purposes, including wooden nickels, pill boxes, beads, buckets, and stamp boxes. The catalog is fun, and the prices are reasonable.

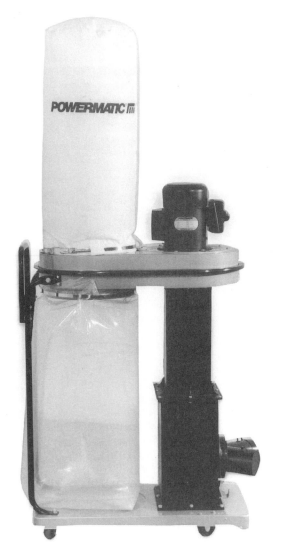

Powermatic's dust collector gives power and easy movement from machine to machine.

RBINDUSTRIES, INC.

1801 Vine St.	(800) 487-2623
P.O. Box 369	(816) 884-3534
Harrisonville MO 64701	FAX: (816) 884-2463

The RBI Hawk line of scroll saws is a good starting point for the tools made and sold by RBIndustries. These American-made scroll saws are among the best to be found, with throat capacities from 14" to 26", with the top three (of four) models produced as free-standing tools. RBI provides a complete line of scroll saw accessories, including a blade rack, diamond blades (for cutting glass and similar hard materials), and a drip tank system for cooling the diamond blade. RBI produces wood planers and a related tool they call the Panel Master, plus a drum sander 38" across, molding accessories for planers (the RBI planers can also be adapted as drum sanders and gang saws), dust collectors, a router table, and two versions of their Router Shop for producing dovetail, mortise and tenon, and other joints. Their catalog is free, and worth looking at. RBI sells by mail, as well as through other retail outlets.

RBI Woodplaner.

RBI Hawk scroll saw.

RECORD TOOLS, INC.

1915 Clements Rd. #1	In U.S.: (800) 267-8367
Pickering ONT	In Canada: (800) 263-7512
Canada L1W 3V1	(416) 428-1077

Record is a leading maker of lathes and turning tools, woodturning workbenches, and varied woodturning accessories, but also turns out a considerable line of top grade hand tools and accessories. Record planes, chisels and turning gouges, skew chisels, and scrapers are famous worldwide for quality, as is the Marples line of chisels, turning and carving tools made in Sheffield, England, since 1828. The Record line of woodworking vises is justly famed, and other tools in the Record line include hammers (a major source of Warrington — cross peen — hammers), clamps, and some wrenches. Record lathes are quality tools, covering a wide range of sizes, from the single end bowl lathe, with a 22" turning capacity, to the Coronet #3, with a 48" distance between centers and a 12" diameter swing over the bed (the #3 takes an accessory set that allows a massive 30" diameter bowl turning). Call or drop a note for information, or check your local or mail-order woodworking tool supplier.

ROUSSEAU COMPANY

1712 13th St.   (800) 635-3416
Clarkston WA 99403   FAX: (509) 758-4991

Call or write for information on the Router-Miter MultiStand.

RUST-OLEUM

11 Hawthorn Parkway
Vernon Hills IL 60061   (800) 323-3584

Rust-Oleum presents Wood Saver, plus a wide line of aerosol paints.

RYOBI AMERICAN CORP.

1424 Pearman Dairy Rd.
Anderson SC 29625   (800) 323-4615

Ryobi calls their line of power tools the Workaholics. The company makes a wide variety of products, from printing equipment through lawn and garden products to hardware and sporting goods, but probably the most relevant other line is a die casting company that has helped them produce lightweight aluminum castings for most of their tools. Ryobi makes bench-top tools and portable power tools, including a remarkable 10" bench-top table saw system (the BT3000) that really expands the concept of the lightweight table saw. From there, you find a scroll saw, a portable radial arm saw, several miter and compound miter saws, a 10" portable planer (this tool was the founder of the current craze for lightweight planers), a 12" portable planer, a jointer-planer, cordless tools, a random orbit sander, belt and part-sheet sanders, drills, circular saws, jig saws, routers and laminate trimmers, power hand planers, a biscuit joiner, and more, until you finally reach stationary tools. Ryobi produces two bandsaws, a chisel mortiser and a chain mortiser, a 12½" planer and a 12½" planer-jointer as stationary tools. The Ryobi mini-catalog is free on request.

SAFETY SPEED CUT MANUFACTURING CO.

13460 N. Hwy. 65
Anoka MN 55304   (612) 755-1600

For years in the past, and very likely for years to come, I have wanted a plywood cutting panel saw such as those manufactured by SSC. There are features no hobby woodworker really needs, all of which tend to add to the cost, and these tools are expensive. But the lower cost models are dropping to within reason as time goes on (or my sense of the dollar's value is getting as warped as a politician's). Most of these are single purpose machines that do nothing beyond ripping and crosscutting plywood. If you use much plywood, however, the savings in time, materials, and energy, and the additions to safety, are quickly obvious. The least expensive

model will take an 8' long panel at normal (48") width, and let you rip or crosscut with the panel in a vertical position. That means you are not feeding the heavy, unwieldy plywood panel into a table saw with all that does for inaccurate and unsafe cutting. The only other option is to use a circular saw to cut nearly to size, and then to finish cut on the table saw — this is what I usually do. It wastes material. Most of us use one or both of the above methods, but if you do a great deal of plywood work, give SSC a call or drop them a note and ask for their catalog.

SANDVIK CONSUMER TOOLS DIVISION

P.O. Box 2036   (800) 632-7297
Scranton PA 18501-1220   FAX: (800) 877-5687

Sandvik's small U.S. marketing division is not exactly eager for calls and letters asking for catalogs, so I suggest you try your local tool supplier first. They offer a fine line of chisels, coping and fret saws, and hand saws, including new hardpoint styles, hammers, and files.

Above and bottom right: Sandvik's wood chisel sets.

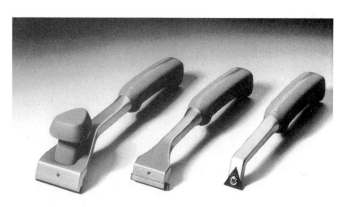

Both types of Sandvik planers are marvelous tools.

SANSHER CORPORATION

8005 N. Clinton St.
Fort Wayne IN 46825   (219) 484-2000

Sansher Corporation offers Dad's Drip Strip latex paint cleaner that also removes polyurethanes, lacquers, shellacs, varnishes, acrylics, paints, and epoxies. The remover is said to cut and dissolve like a liquid, while lifting and staying wet like a semi-gel, so that the stripping job may be stopped at any time, without waste or damage, for later resumption. It comes with its own chemical resistant sprayer, doesn't need a neutralizer, and is washed off with plain water, leaving no residue. I have not used this particular brand of remover, but if it does most of what is claimed, it will reduce work, odor, and mess considerably. Call or write the company for a brochure.

SARAL PAPER COMPANY

322 W. 57th St.
Suite 30
New York NY 10019

Saral makes a wax-free transfer paper for getting plans from your drawings to your wood.

SAVOGRAN

P.O. Box 130
Norwood MA 02062   (800) 225-9872

Savogran markets a really good and non-polluting paint-brush cleaner — CleanSafer. Call or write for information.

Dad's Easy Spray Paint, Stain & Varnish Remover.

SEARS, ROEBUCK & CO.

Check with your local Sears retail store, or call (800) 377-7414 for their free tool catalog. Featuring their own Craftsman tool line, Sears also presents power tools from many other manufacturers, including Ryobi, Makita, Black & Decker, and Skil.

Craftsman's Rout-A-Copier is a guide system for routers.

Craftsman air-powered staplers are very useful for woodworkers.

Sears now has a router pad to reduce the need for vises and clamps, which are always difficult to use with small workpieces.

SECO INVESTMENTS COMPANY

315 Cloverleaf Dr. #C   (818) 333-1799
Baldwin Park CA 91706   FAX: (818) 333-1899

Seco manufactures and distributes primarily heavy-duty woodworking machinery, much of which is not going to interest hobby woodworkers. There are a number of exceptions, including a broad line of dust collectors from a 1 horse single phase unit up to a 10 horse three phase. Depending on the price, the 20" bandsaw might be of interest to some hobbyists, and they also have a good-looking (in the catalog) 10" table saw — 3 horsepower and single phase. Most of the rest of the machinery will remain as fantasy materials (many woodworkers would love a wide planer, but imagine the work installing the 5 horse, single phase 770 pound 20"). All the 24" models are three phase, which places them well out of the range of hobby shops. Seco also distributes a good-looking line of stock feeders. Literature is free and worth asking for if you have any interest in the heavier woodworking machinery.

SHOPCARTS

445 Harriet St.   (415) 552-9522
San Francisco CA 94103   FAX: (415) 552-9521

The Shopcarts sheet panel handler would have proved very handy in my latest project. I had to slice four ¾" thick panels of oak plywood and another of ½" pine, plus a sixth of ¼" lauan. Unfortunately, the shop I'm using is too small for that sort of equipment, as handy as it is. For the home workshop, probably the most useful item made and sold by Shopcarts is the Panel Skate. This is a small unit (it weighs five pounds and is a foot long) with a V placed between four wheels. This aluminum alloy V gives a 3" angle hold, and when centered (or nearly so) will let you roll a pretty good-sized sheet around the shop with almost no effort. I will be getting one for my shop very soon. Shopcarts' literature is free.

Shopcarts' panel handler.

Shopcarts' parts cart.

Shopcarts' Panel Skate.

SHOP-VAC CORP.

2323 Reach Rd.
Williamsport PA 17701-0307

Drop Shop-Vac a note and ask for catalog material on their justly famous line of shop vacuums, to which they have recently added the ToolMate shop cleaner. The ToolMate offers two-stage filtering as it picks up directly from your tool's outlet (the ToolMate has a 4" diameter inlet to fit most standard tool dust outlets). The 1.25 horse ToolMate, however, is not nearly as powerful as some Shop-Vacs, which run up to three horsepower in both industrial and home models.

SHOPSMITH, INC.

3931 Image Dr.	(800) 543-7586
Dayton OH 45414	(513) 898-6070

Shopsmith tools take minimal space and quickly convert to different tools: the base unit works as a table saw, lathe, vertical drill press, and horizontal borer.

SIMPSON STRONG-TIE COMPANY, INC.

1450 Doolittle Dr.
P.O. Box 1568   (800) 227-1562
San Leandro CA 94577   FAX: (510) 562-7946

A company with framing anchors as a primary product may seem a strange inclusion for a woodworkers' source book, but Simpson's line includes some items of definite interest: Rigid-Tie corner connectors, for example, work well to ease the assembly of benches and materials' holders, while shelf brackets can save much installation time in creating shop storage. Drop a card to Simpson and request information on either do-it-yourself or RTC materials or both.

SINGLEY SPECIALTY CO., INC.

P.O. Box 5087
Greensboro NC 27403   (919) 852-8581

This company makes sleeveless drum sanders. Send a self-addressed, stamped envelope for a list.

SKIL CORPORATION

4300 W. Peterson Ave.
Chicago IL 60646

Skil Corporation will send a copy of its full color 80+-page full lines catalog to readers for $1.00. Skilsaw has become

Simpson Strong-Tie corner connectors help make this workbench.

almost a generic term for circular saw (which the company fights like the devil, of course). It is flattering to be so closely associated with a tool your company brought out first, but in later years it's also limiting. In recent years, Skil Corporation is noted for a full line of corded and cordless portable power tools, and has recently developed a full line of bench-top stationary tools: a table saw, a drill press, a disc/belt sander, a scroll saw, a bench grinder. Their Top Gun 12 volt cordless drill is accepted as one of the top models in that field. The new Skil all ball bearing random orbit sander also fits in well with woodworking needs. New random orbit disc sanders are excellent finish sanders, but can get down and hog off the wood with some lighter duty belt sanders when pushed.

Skil's benchtop belt/disc sander is very handy in small shops.

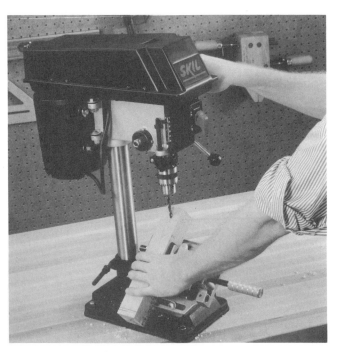

Skil's benchtop drill press does most of the jobs a floor unit will do, though without the huge capacity and high price.

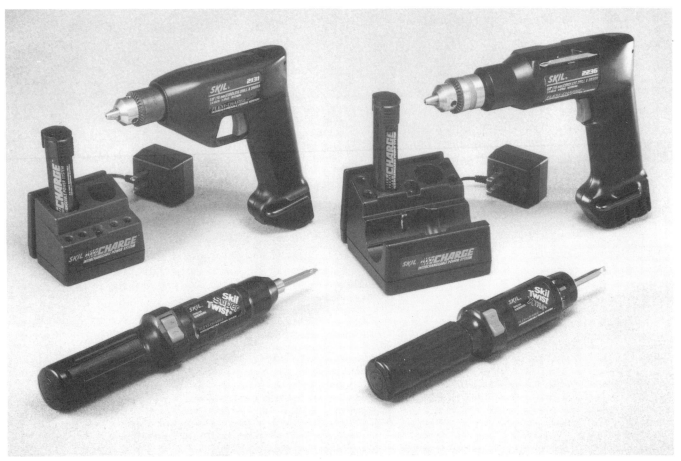

Skil's Flexi-Charge cordless tool series all use the same 3.6 volt battery packs, but one tool, the 7.2 volt driver-drill, uses two packs in series.

SONIN, INC.

672 White Plains Rd.   (800) 223-7511
Scarsdale NY 10583   In NY state: (914) 725-0202
                            (914) 725-1158

Sonin produces high tech linear measuring tools, plumbs, levels, and a new moisture test meter and moisture test tool. These electronic tools give a very rapid indication of moisture present, with the meter measuring levels from 10 to 28%. Sonin also makes various electronic and non-electronic distance measuring tools, including measuring tapes, and circuit testers that may prove handy around the workshop.

STANLEY DOOR SYSTEMS

1225 East Maple Rd.   (313) 528-2500
Troy MI 48084   FAX: (313) 528-1424

Call or write for brochures on Stanley doors, used in garages, residences, shops, and everywhere else.

STANLEY FASTENING SYSTEMS

Route 2, Briggs Dr.   (401) 884-2500
East Greenwich RI 02818   FAX: (401) 884-2485

Stanley-Bostitch air nailers are handy even in the home workshop. Most useful are the brad and finishing nailers. The company also makes their own line of small air compressors. Call or write for information.

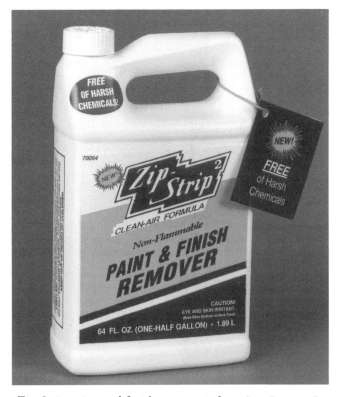

Zip-Strip paint and finish remover is from Star Bronze Co.

STANLEY HARDWARE

480 Myrtle St.   (203) 225-5111
New Britain CT 06053   (203) 827-5729

Call or write for information on Stanley Hardware items. You may want, to save time, to check the full line catalog at your hardware store, for Stanley makes a line of solid brass hardware that's great for woodworking projects.

STANLEY TOOLS

600 Myrtle St.   (203) 225-5111
New Britain CT 06050   FAX: (203) 827-5829

Anyone not at least minimally familiar with the Stanley tool line has been on another planet for the past hundred-plus years. Call or write for further information on hammers, screwdrivers, planes, chisels, awls, nail sets, and much, much more.

STAR BRONZE COMPANY

803 South Mahoning
Alliance OH 44601   (800) 321-9870

At the above number, ask for Nancy Hentsch in Customer Service.

Along with Zip-Guard urethane Wood Finish, Star Bronze manufactures sanding eliminators, furniture refinishers, Zip-Strip paint and finish remover for water cleanup, interior and exterior wood stains and wood preservative, plus Dekorator's Enamel in two-ounce bottles. On request, they will send a free copy of their extensive booklet "Refinishing and Finishing." The booklet provides good general information and also details the use of many Star Bronze products.

The Kiddiehaus was built following directions from The Stanley Works and using Stanley Tools. The booklet with the plan is "Building Wooden Toys."

STEUSS CREATIONS

334 Atherton Ave.
Novato CA 94945　　　　　　　　(415) 897-1457

Steuss has designed the Eze-Angleguide for radial arm saws. Call or write for further information.

SUGINO CORP.

1700 N. Penny Lane
Schaumburg IL 60173　　　　　　(708) 397-9401

Sugino Corporation will send free information on the Auto Mach power wood carving tool.

SUNHILL NIC CO., INC.

500 Andover Park East
Seattle WA 98188　　　　　　　(800) 544-1361

Sunhill imports power feeders, dust collectors, table saws, jointers, planers, and bandsaws under several brand names, with some machines aimed at the commercial market, unless your shop budget can afford a $3700 10" oscillating edge sander, or a 7.5 horse, three phase, 24" x 9" surface planer at $5650, or maybe a four head 6" x 2¼" molder at $9985. In fairness, they also bring in a $389 6" jointer, and a 12" portable planer for the same price, as well as moderate and low cost band saws, table saws, and other tools. Write or call for their latest brochure.

TASHIRO'S

1024 S. Bailey St.
Seattle WA 98108　　　　　　　(206) 762-8242

Tashiro's has been importing Japanese tools for over a century, and offers a solid array of saw blades and handles for almost all wood-cutting purposes. The catalog is free, and contains instruction on selecting the right blade for the job and using the proper handle for the blades needed.

TAYLOR DESIGN GROUP

P.O. Box 810262　　　　　　　(214) 243-7943
Dallas TX 75381　　　　　FAX: (214) 243-4277

This design group is the maker of Incra jigs, which present the best method of producing finger joints I have ever used or heard of, when combined with a good router table. Sooner or later I will get a chance to check their new professional model, with its larger fence and aluminum (rather than plastic) construction. The line of tools and accessories includes Incra Mike, a master template library, a Miter Slider (runners to allow you to make many table saw jigs), and wooden hinge plans. This is not the entire line, for there is a variety of accessories for the jigs, and a video as well as the template book. A brochure describing the entire line is free for the asking, and you will find it well worth looking over.

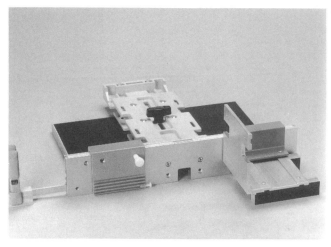

The original Incra Jig, with an 18" fence system and an Incra Right Angle fixture.

TCM INDUSTRIES, INC.

322 Paseo Sonrisa
Walnut CA 91789　　　　　　　(714) 594-0780

TCM is an importer of power woodworking tools. Call or write for details.

TECO/LUMBERLOK

Box 203　　　　　　Orders: (800) 638-8989
Colliers Way　　　Technical: (800) 438-8326
Colliers WV 26035　　　　FAX: (304) 797-7302

Teco/Lumberlok
P.O. Box 55131　　　National: (800) 221-7905
Hayward CA 94545　California: (900) 221-7906
　　　　　　　　　　　　　　　(415) 489-8500
　　　　　　　　　　　　FAX: (415) 489-2650

Teco/Lumberlok fasteners provide many methods for setting up workbenches, shelving, and similar projects. Teco will also provide project brochures, though most should be available through retailers of Teco products. These include projects that may be of interest to woodworkers. The Teco/Lumberlok catalog is also available for a card to either office.

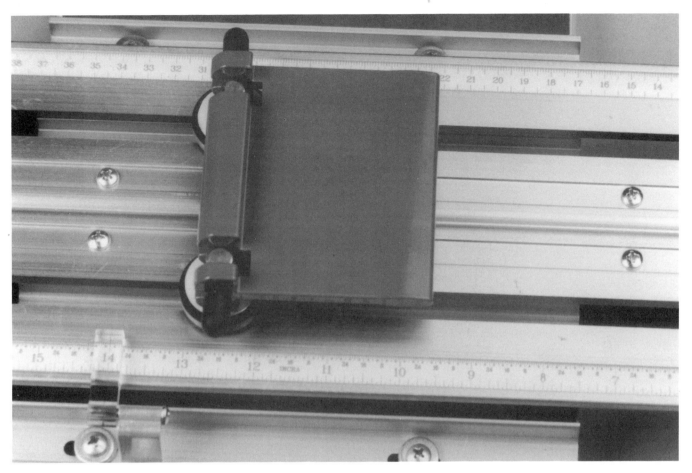

Cam clamp detail on an Incra Jig Pro.

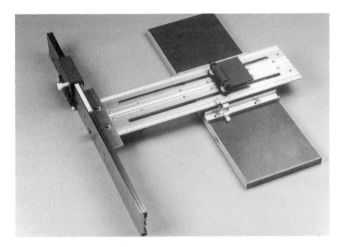

*The Incra Jig Pro (16" model) with a 28"
Incra Pro Fence system.*

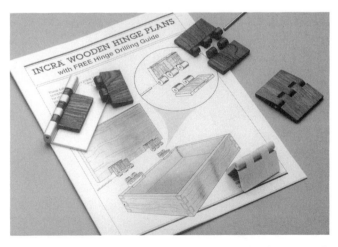

*Wooden Hinge Plans booklet, and some wooden hinges made
from the plans. Courtesy of Taylor Design Group.*

TIP SANDBLAST EQUIPMENT

7075 Rt. 446
P.O. Box 649
Canfield OH 44406   (216) 533-3384

Write for their free catalog of sandblasting equipment.

TOTAL SHOP

P.O. Box 25429
Greenville SC 29616

This tool is similar to the Shopsmith. Write for the free catalog.

TREND-LINES

375 Beacham St.   Catalog request number:
Chelsea MA 02150   (800) 366-6966

Trend-Lines is a discount mail order house, and a distributor of the Reliant line of power tools. Their free catalog

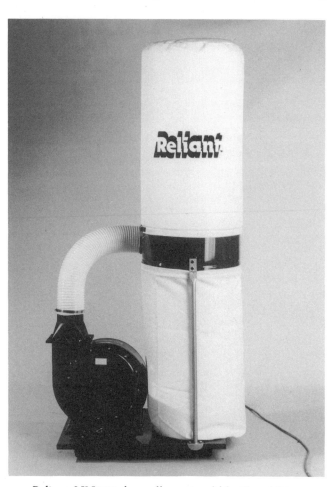

Reliant NN820 dust collector is sold by Trend-Lines.

presents more than 3,000 brand-name products, including power tools and accessories, hand tools, screws, hardware, wood parts, plans, books, and more. All popular brand names are carried, including Black & Decker, Porter-Cable, Milwaukee, Delta, Veritas, Stanley-Bostitch, ITW-Paslode, Campbell-Hausfeld, Makita, Skil, Ryobi, DeWalt, Oldham, Freud, Panasonic, and others. Complete satisfaction guarantee.

TRIMTRAMP, LTD.

151 Carlingview Dr., Unit 11
Etobicoke ONT   (416) 798-3160
Canada M9W 5S4   FAX: (416) 798-3162

Trimtramp's sliding compound miter table gives you a chance to convert your 7¼" or 8¼" circular saw to a compound miter saw at very low cost, compared to the cost of a complete unit. The circular saw lifts out for use as it was originally designed. Cutting action is on the back stroke, reducing splintering, and the cut width max is 16", considerably more than the widest of the compound miter saws I have used. The unit, without saw, weighs only 21 pounds, and may be clamped right on top of a Black & Decker Work-Mate to add further ease of portability. Call, fax, or drop them a note for more information, including prices and where to buy the Trimtramp.

U.S. SAFETY

8101 Lenexa Dr.
Lenexa KS 66215   (913) 599-5555

Write for free information on respirators.

UGL (UNITED GILSONITE LABORATORIES)

P.O. Box 70
Scranton PA 18501   (800) UGL-LABS

Manufacturers of ZAR wood finishing products, including penetrating wood stains; clear polyurethane varnishes in gloss, satin, and flat finishes; and exterior polys in brush-on and spray formulations. Also ZAR Aqua, a new line of clear polyurethanes that are water based, hence cutting odors, flammability dangers, and solvent emissions problems. (These non-yellowing finishes also let you clean up with soap and water, and are formulated for easy brushing. Many of the new water-based polys are formulated primarily for spraying.) ZAR tung oil is a wipe-on (in my experience, an old T-shirt is the best applicator) product that produces a surface resistant to water and most chemicals. Give them a call and they will send a free brochure, "The Finishing Touch."

ZAR Polyurethane is brushed on. Courtesy of UGL.

ZAR wood stain wipes on. Courtesy of UGL.

ZAR Wipe On tung oil goes on best with an old T-shirt and provides a lovely finish. Courtesy of UGL.

UNITED STEEL PRODUCTS

703 Rogers Dr.
Montgomery MN 56069   (800) 328-5934

United Steel makes Kant Sag hardware for building, which is handy if you are constructing shops and similar projects.

VACCON CO., INC.

32 Rear Spring St.
P.O. Box 324
Medfield MA 02052   (800) 848-8788

Call or write for information on vacuum clamping and veneering gear.

VAUGHAN & BUSHNELL MFG. CO.

11414 Maple Ave.   (815) 648-2446
Hebron IL 60034   FAX: (815) 648-4300

Vaughan & Bushnell makes a wide line of striking tools, from hickory-handled claw hammers to rawhide and rubber mallets, and axes and similar items. The line of carpenter's claw hammers is wider than most, with head weights as low as 7 ounces and as heavy as 32 ounces, and including the standard stops at 13, 16, 20, 24, and 28 ounces (I know of no other maker of 7 and 32 ounce claw hammers). Handle materials cover the standard hickory, fiberglass, and tubular and solid steel. The variety of soft-faced hammers, including rawhide, plastics, and rubber, is wide enough to let you drive together any tight joint with no marks on even the softest wood. Send an SASE for information on striking tools and even some struck tools — they make some chisels and many pry bars as well as hammers, axes, sledges, and hatchets.

Vaughan & Bushnell's Superbar is a bar-of-all-work and does a great many jobs around any shop.

VEGA

Rural Route 3
Decatur IL 62526   (800) 222-VEGA

Vega makes a line of accessories that is unusual in design concept and useful, including an aftermarket table saw fence and a truly efficient miter gauge. Call or write for information.

VELVIT PRODUCTS COMPANY

P.O. Box 1741
Appleton WI 54913   (414) 722-8355

Velvit's Chemgard wood treatments include Velvit oil interior finish, Chemgard wood treatments (for wood and logs that won't be sealed for months), and Cabin & Deck Finish for exterior work. Call or write for information.

Vaughan & Bushnell's 10 ounce head weight Little Pro hammer is exceptionally handy for light work.

VERITAS TOOLS

12 E. River St.   (613) 596-1922
Ogdensburg NY 13669   Office: (613) 596-0350
                      FAX: (613) 596-3073

The variety of interesting and useful tools that comes from Veritas is close to astounding. At the outset, there is a tendency to think of less expensive formed plastic tools, such as the center marker, the tool setting gauge, and the poly gauge.

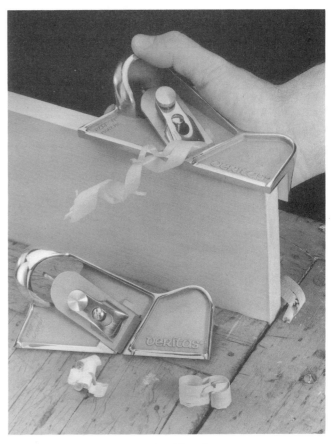

Veritas shoulder plane.

Veritas shelf pin drilling guide.

Veritas burnishers.

That notion quickly slides away as you note, on moving away from the pair of simple corner rounding tools to the edge trimming block plane, and the Veritas shelf drilling jig at over $100.00, or the Tucker vise, at $495.00. The Tucker vise may need some justification, other than its 13" wide jaws, 4" throat, 5½" wide side jaws with 4½" throat, 2¾" wide carver's chop jaws with 6" throat depth, double ⅞" guide rods, and 12" opening for all jaws; so consider it allows full rotation and tilt, has integral dogs (four 6" round dogs: two in each jaw), pivoting front jaw, automatic opening, quick-release, lined jaws (cork), elevated guide rods, and much more. It is, in fact, the epitome of current woodworkers' vises. Whether or not it's worth 500 bucks depends on

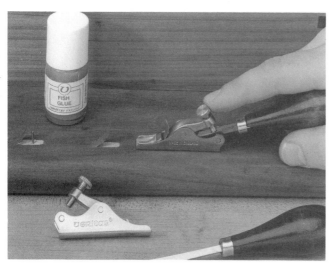

Veritas nail hiding plane and fish glue are used to completely hide nail heads.

Veritas edge rounders are most useful on soft woods but will work well with the grain on most hardwoods.

your needs and wants. (*Popular Mechanics* presented the Tucker Vise with its Design and Engineering award in January 1992.)

VERMONT-AMERICAN TOOL COMPANY

P.O. Box 340
Lincolnton NC 28093-0340   (704) 735-7464

Vermont-American is a full line tool accessory company that manufactures saw blades, drill bits, and many other items. Call or write for free information.

WAGNER FINECOAT

1770 Fernbrook Lane   (800) 328-8251
Plymouth MN 55447   In MN: (612) 553-7000

For many years, Wagner has been a primary source of airless paint sprayers and power roll-on painters. Now they produce one of a new array of low cost HVLP (high volume, low pressure) sprayers in addition to their other models. HVLP sprayers work with four pounds per square inch of air, instead of the up to 2,500 PSI conventional systems use. The first real difference you will note on seeing one is the diameter of the air supply hose: it is about three times as large as that of conventional air hoses. HVLP now offers low cost equipment, low overspray, and general ease of use whether

Wagner FineCoat HVLP (high volume, low pressure) spray system.

for clear finish coats or heavier paints. Such sprayers are ideal for the new water-based poly finishes. Call or write for free information.

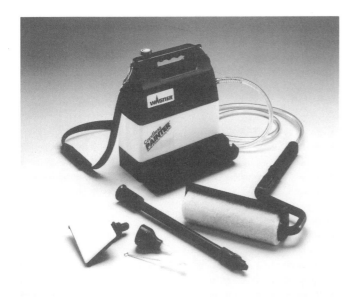

Wagner cordless painter.

WARREN TOOL COMPANY

2209-1 Rt. 9G
Rhinebeck NY 12572   (914) 876-7817

Fred Clark offers a multiplicity of carving tools, with interchangeable blades for the many handles, and a variety of kits. Warren Tool also carries sharpening tools for most carving implements, books, sharpening accessories, and related tools. Fred's operation is both wholesale and retail. You may wish to check to determine your possible eligibility for wholesaling this line. The catalog is $1.00.

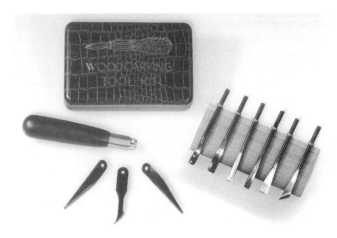

Wood carving kit from Warren Tool.

WEN PRODUCTS, INC.

5810 Northwest Hwy.
Chicago IL 60631   (312) 763-6060

Wen is an old company that makes some portable power tools. Call or write for details.

WILKE MACHINERY COMPANY

3230 Susquehanna Trail   (717) 764-5000
York PA 17402   FAX: (717) 764-3778

Bridgewood woodworking machinery is featured in the Wilke catalog and starts with an emphasis on the big guns, their 24" x 9" planer being the lead-off item. At a net weight of 1,910 pounds, this might go through the floor in more than a few shops I know. A few pages on, we run into small shop tools with a 20" economy planer (still 771 pounds),

Warren carving knife, blades, and a tiny carved figure.

Wilke's Bridgewood lathe.

then to the 15" planer, and on to the 12" portable model (64 pounds net). Throughout, there is a choice of huge, medium, and small shop items (except for those items that aren't at all suitable to small shops, such as 4-side moulders, and 3-side planer-moulders, tenoners and so on. The current sale price on the Bridgewood 20½" floor drill press is a stunner. The catalog is $1.00 (free in the showroom) and well worth checking out.

Zinsser amber Bulls Eye shellac.

Wilke's Bridgewood 10" table saw.

WILLIAM ZINSSER & CO.

39 Belmont Dr., Dept. WSB
Somerset NJ 08875   (908) 469-8100

Zinsser Bulls Eye Shellac Sealer & Finish comes in a standard three pound cut, in white and orange (they now call these clear and amber), in half-pints, pints, quarts, gallons, and five-gallon buckets. This is not a mail order item so is found in home centers and hardware stores, but the company will send a free brochure describing the products and their uses. Shellac makes a superb one-coat undercoat for wallpaper, and the wallpaper strips off easily when the time comes for a change. Spackled areas sealed with shellac do not need several coats of paint to kill the flat look. Knots and sap streaks in new wood are nicely sealed with shellac, and woods such as pine take paint more evenly when first given a coat of shellac. Shellac has a lot of good points as a clear finish too, points we often forget these days. Drop a card to William Zinsser & Company and get an idea of what some of those good points are. Or be reminded if, like me, you used to know.

Zinsser white Bulls Eye shellac.

WILLIAMS & HUSSEY MACHINE CO., INC.

Riverview Mill   (800) 258-1380
P.O. Box 1149   (603) 654-6828
Wilton NH 03086   FAX: (603) 654-5446

The W&H molder-planer unit offers quick blade changes and a capacity of almost double blade width because one side is open, allowing double pass cutting. The unit also takes moulding cutting blades, to double utility. The W&H lathe is relatively low cost and high precision. Write or call for free information kit.

JOHN WILSON

500 E. Broadway Hwy.
Charlotte MI 48813   (517) 543-5325

John is the modern day torch bearer for Shaker oval boxes and offers everything from instruction sheets to the kits to make the boxes, right up to and including the correct kind of copper nails for the bands. A typical Shaker oval box kit will include materials for the lid, box bands (to be bent to shape), and wood for the bottom, plus an instruction sheet. You add wood glue, a saw that will cut an oval, 120 and 220 grit sandpaper, and clear finish. He has his own video, and

John Wilson is surrounded by his Shaker boxes.
Photo by Dan Fink.

a line of tools, accessories, and patterns that makes the overall job a great deal simpler. John also has a pattern packet that presents more than two dozen oval boxes and carriers, and he offers workshops at specific intervals during the year, and at varied places, so you don't always have to be in Michigan to learn to make oval boxes. Give him a call, or drop a note, to check prices of current literature and workshops.

WOODCRAFT

210 Wood County Industrial Park   (800) 225-1153
P.O. Box 1686   Customer service: (800) 535-4482
Parkersburg WV 26102-1686   Technical advice:
                                     (800) 535-4486

Woodcraft has been around for a long time, starting in 1928. Their catalog is second in attractiveness to Garrett Wade's only because the photography is a touch less lush, slanting more to information presentation in top grade photographs, without exotic lighting. It is just as colorful, just as well photographed, and there are many unusual items, including Sorby's ring cutting tools, six lathe tools that make the turning of captive rings (rings turned on a shaft and left trapped inside end pieces on that shaft) easy even for novices. The process is normally one that needs a great deal of practice with skews and parting tools. Woodcraft emphasizes carving tools more than any other general woodworking catalog I am familiar with, and offers project supplies (hardwood dowels, plugs, wheels, etc.), a wide variety of finishing products, bits and other boring tools, some small power tools (Carba-Tec miniature lathe, Delta 12" portable planer, Delta 2 speed 16" scroll saw), and a bunch of router and other power tool accessories, including the Incra Pro jig series. Specific tool brands, such as the Lynx saw from Sheffield, England's Garlick Saw Company, are offered. This handsaw is nearly labor intensive enough in manufacture to truly deserve the name "handmade" that it is given. Lie-Nielsen reproduction tools are featured in the plane section, though the Clifton Multiplane takes the honor box: this very, very expensive hand plane with its interchangeable blades offers a 100-year-old tradition for handmade tongue and groove joints, beading, fillisters, ovolos, rounds, dadoes, rabbets, and many others. This is another catalog well worth its cost, in this case, $3.00.

WOOD-MET SERVICES

3314 W. Shoff
Peoria IL 61604   (309) 637-4667

Wood-Met has passed its tenth anniversary, and Norwood Snowden sent me a pile of material to show how useful the 700 or so plans that are included in his $1.00 (refundable) catalog actually are. No argument there, with over eighty attachments for lathes, drill presses, and routers. The preponderance of Wood-Met Services' plans tends to lean to the metal working, but there are more than enough wood-working tool and accessory plans to make the catalog worthwhile. Shop equipment, portable power tools, and accessories such as a mobile wood lathe tool holder are very useful. Plans are small scale, but clear and nicely dimensioned. Instructions are clear. Snowden spent forty-one years with Caterpillar design, research, and development before retiring and starting Wood-Met.

WOOD-MIZER PRODUCTS, INC.

8180 W. 10th St.   (800) 553-0182
Indianapolis IN 46214   (317) 271-1542

Wood-Mizer is your company if you are truly sick of paying high prices for good lumber. The company makes portable sawmills of the bandsaw type (generally a bit lower in cost—though far from inexpensive for the good ones, which this is — than circular sawmill setups, as well as being more portable). There are six versions, and the catalog then goes on to describe Solar Dry kilns to finish up the work. Actually, the smallest Solar Dry kiln is not wildly expensive (again, it depends on your state of interest and wallet: delivered, it will probably run about $2,250, with a current price of $2,090), and will dry 750 board feet at a time. The third product line is the Dupli-Carver used to produce three-dimensional wood carving duplicates. The catalog is free and fascinating.

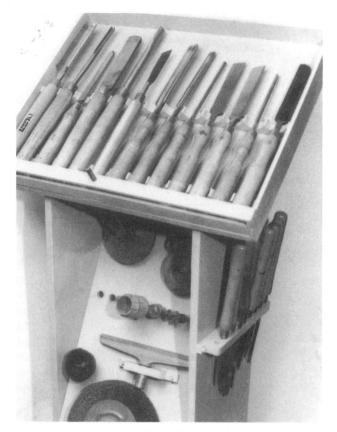

Lathe tool stand made from Wood-Met plan set #160.

Wood-Mizer bandsaw saw mill.

WOODCARE PRODUCTS

3548 Riverdale Rd.   (800) 676-GLUE
Ogden UT 84405   (801) 393-3900

Call or write for free information on adhesives.

WOODHAVEN

5323 W. Kimberly   (800) 344-6657
Davenport IA 52806   (319) 391-2386

Woodhaven is a fairly old (past a decade) mail order house for router bits, tables, and general router supplies. Their router base plate is offered in four basic styles and may be modified to fit jig saws in one style. Inlay templates for construction of your own router table tops are also offered, as are fences, angle brackets, and a slew of interesting items for the router-using woodworker. The Woodhaven miter and box joint jig is a neat item, from appearances and reports. For dowel-making jigs, vacuum clamp kits, Keller dovetailing jigs, Beall wood threaders, and an array of other items, this catalog offers much of interest to the woodworker. One such item is the Know-Bit. This is not much more than a pointed metal dowel, with the point set to the top when inserted in a router. It then serves as an exact centering device for router, drill press, and lathe. It is machined perfectly straight and round, so it also makes a good run-out (wobble) check when used with a dial indica-tor. Chuck it into your drill press, router, or lathe and quickly and simply measure the run-out. The catalog is free by bulk mail, $3.00 first class.

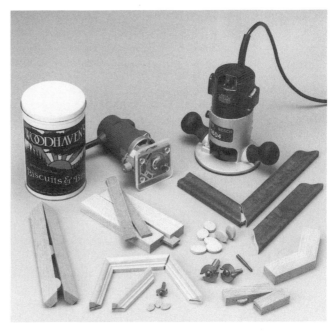

Woodhaven offers a really special biscuit joining kit for routers.

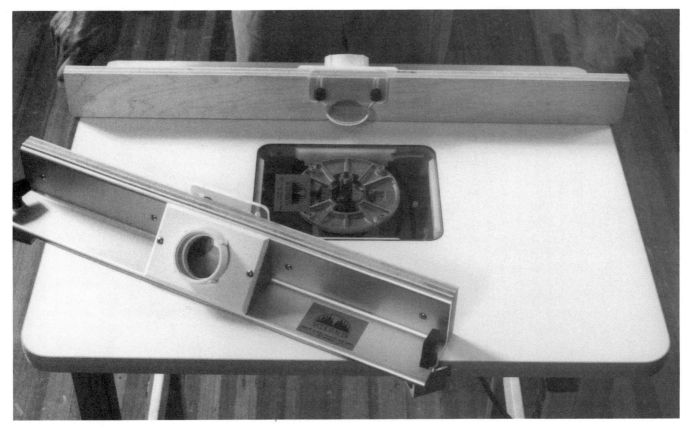

Woodhaven's router table looks superb.

WOODMASTER TOOLS

2908 Oak
Kansas City MO 64108

Woodmaster power feed machines include drum sanders to 38" wide, and combination sander/molder/planer/saw units to 25" wide. Information is free.

WOODS WIRE PRODUCTS

510 3rd Ave. S.W.
P.O. Box 2675   (800) 428-6168
Carmel IN 46032   (317) 844-7261

Call or write for information on add-on ground fault circuit interrupters. GFCIs are always worthwhile additions to shop circuitry, as they stop electrical shocks before the shock can harm a healthy person.

WOODSTOCK INTERNATIONAL, INC.

P.O. Box 2027   (206) 734-3482
Bellingham WA 98227   (206) 671-3053

Woodstock International does *not* sell direct to consumers, so if you have an urge to look over their lines of dust collector accessories (blast gates, connectors, etc.), rub collars, and vise clamps, get your dealer to call for a catalog. For a quick look at the line, write and ask for their product brochure that shows the Rebel router table, router table inserts, rosette cutterheads, and other items.

Woodstock's Rebel router table.

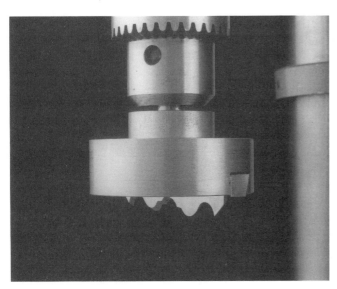

Woodstock's rosette cutter.

YORK SAW & KNIFE COMPANY, INC.

P.O. Box 733
York PA 17405   (800) OK4-SAWS

Call or write for information on their Luxite carbide saw blades.

SECTION III

MAIL ORDER SOURCES

A.R.E. MANUFACTURING, INC.

518 S. Springbrook Rd.
Newberg OR 97132 (800) 541-4962

The Correct Cut radial arm saw fence replaces the existing fence, provides a precise measuring scale, and has a built-in hinged stop. It is available in any length. Call or write for further information.

ADAMS WOOD PRODUCTS

974 Forest Dr. (615) 587-2942
Morristown TN 37814 FAX: (615) 586-2188

The Adams catalog (free) shows legs for projects from Queen Anne to tapered in enough detail to make me wish one of my current or immediately upcoming projects needed such legs. Stock items include Queen Anne legs, table bases, table and chair kits, in walnut, cherry, oak, mahogany, and maple. Carved knees may be added to many Queen Anne legs, as may claw and ball feet. Bun and tapered feet are also available. Prices vary widely, depending on your needs. Obviously, more costly woods mean more costly parts, as do longer and larger parts. Leg length varies from 8" to 29½", with a box of forty-eight for the smaller legs and a box of a dozen for the longer. Part box prices are the highest, so if you foresee using a dozen long legs over the years, buy the box and save a bit over 10 percent. Turned table legs are less costly, until you get into fluted types, of which Adams Wood Products carries a wide variety. The catalog is interesting, and the idea of not having to bandsaw Queen Anne-style legs makes the prices very reasonable. Overall, the products open out the project possibilities for those of us without bandsaws and lathes. Oak table columns and feet are available too, and some items may now be made of mesquite.

AIRSTREAM DUST HELMETS

Hwy. 54 South (800) 328-1792
P.O. Box 975 (218) 685-4457
Elbow Lake MN 56531 FAX: (218) 685-4458

Airstream is the distributor for the Racal line of lung and eye protection helmets — respirators — that provide protection from dust, lacquers, glues, and strippers. The company also distributes hearing protectors, safety glasses, and a negative (no air pump) respirator for those who don't wish to pay the cost of the positive (pumped air) systems. The catalog is available at no charge, on request. Airstream sells through its own mail order company.

ALLIANCE ABRASIVES, INC.

23649 SR 62
P.O. Box 3447
Alliance OH 44601 (800) 873-7957

Call or write for a free list of sanding belts and similar abrasive tools.

AMERICAN CLOCKMAKER

Box 326
Clintonville WI 54929
(800) 236-7300

Write or call for their free catalog of clock kits.

AMERICAN MACHINE & TOOL COMPANY

Fourth Ave. and Spring St. (215) 948-0400
Royersford PA 19468-2519 Orders: (800) 435-8665
Customer service, parts, inquiries: (800) 435-3279

American Machine & Tool Company distributes, by mail order, tools made to its own specifications in Taiwan. The AMT line of low to moderate cost tools and their range of accessories is shown in a free catalog. Over time, I have used AMT lathes and drill presses, plus a number of accessories, and found them excellent representatives of the moderate price scale for power tools. I have not had a chance to use their newer lines of hand tools and accessories but expect they will be on a par with the other lines. The drill press accepts a wide variety of accessories, all also sold by AMT.

AMERIGLAS

P.O. Box 27668
Omaha NE 68127

AmeriGlas charges $1.00 for their stained glass catalog. The catalog covers tools, materials, books, videos, lamps, bevels, and a great deal more.

ANNE'S CALICO CAT ORIGINALS

Box 1004
Oakdale CA 95361

For $1.00, Anne Engert will send a catalog of crafting patterns and cutouts, all of cats. From the color photos Anne sent, the patterns are attractive and the cuts very nicely done. The CAT-alog, as Anne calls it, brings with it a $2.00 off coupon for your first order. She will also supply a sample plan packet for $3.00, the plan to be one of her choice.

ANTIQUE HARDWARE STORE

RD 2, Box A   (800) 422-9982
Kintnersville PA 18930   (215) 847-2447

The Antique Hardware Store features cast iron and brass hardware reproductions for cabinets, ice boxes, bathrooms, kitchens, general household doors, and other rooms. Of greatest interest to woodworkers, cabinet hardware includes some hard-to-find items of reproduction Victoriana, plus some more standard items, including different kinds of Chippendale pulls, bail pulls, porcelain knobs, escutcheons, knobs, and drop pulls. Tim Judge says his catalog is free to readers, and it's well worth looking through, both for woodworking related items and for curiosities such as the pillbox toilet.

ARCH DAVIS DESIGN

P.O. Box 119
Morrill ME 04952   (207) 342-4055

Arch forced me to work more by sending me his book on making raised panels on a table saw (*The Raised Panel Book*, $9.95 plus $2.00 shipping) and a booklet on knowing wood moisture content ($2.00, postage and handling included). I quickly found the title description of the panel book was a bit light, as Arch covers most methods of making such panels

and the doors in which they are normally included, for many different applications from cabinets to household doors. He includes several interesting projects as well. In essence, the booklet on wood moisture content shows how to use a vernier caliper to determine moisture content. It's a bit complex and time consuming compared to sticking a meter's probes into the wood, but should be accurate. Arch Davis also sells plans for a lobster boat and a sailboat, and is aiming to have three more plan packages ready shortly. Drop a note for his price list. The plans, of which he sent me a couple of sheets, are nicely done too.

ARMOR

Box 445   (800) 292-8296
East Northport NY 11731   (516) 462-6228
                                  FAX: (516) 462-5793

John Capotosto writes that, for my readers, he is reducing the standard $1.00 catalog price to zero. That was the second nice surprise in John's package. The 72-page catalog is not just of plans, but contains many small tools, finishes, furniture trim, hardware, and other items, plus four pages of books (in which John has forgone the temptation to include mostly his and brother Rosario's woodworking titles, of which there are many). The book selection, like the plan selection, is very wide for the number of books listed. Clock

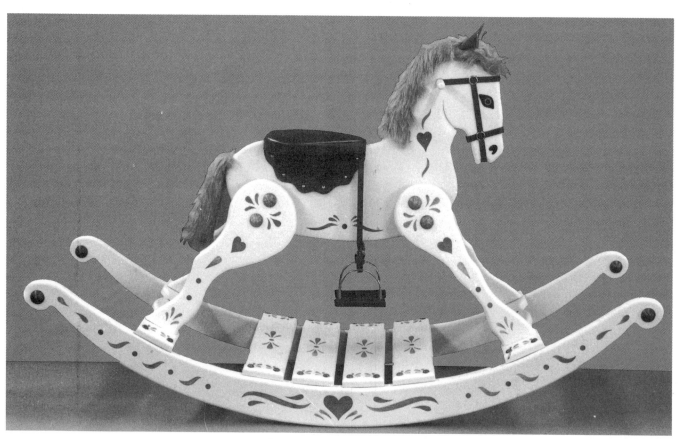

Armor design #400 rocking horse plans will bring joy to many a child.

plans range from a 77" Washington Hall Clock to a simple outline-cut cowboy boot clock. John also offers a classic roll-top desk plan (with or without his parts kit), cheval mirror, gun cabinets, dry sinks, workbenches, tea carts, cradles, desks, children's outdoor furniture, billiard tables, table soccer plans, lamp plans, rocking horses, toys, vehicles, doll houses (including kits), and more. Many of the plans are developments from John's articles in top do-it-yourself and craft magazines over the years and are well worth reviewing. The catalog is a must see.

BADGER HARDWOODS

Route 1, Box 262
Walworth WI 53184   (800) 252-2373

Select or better hardwoods are listed in Badger's free catalog, as are 20 board foot special packs (current prices, per board foot: red elm, $1.55; hard maple, $1.49; walnut, $3.05).

BALL AND BALL

463 W. Lincoln Hwy.
Exton PA 19341   (215) 363-7330

The Ball and Ball reproduction hardware catalog is $5.00 (108 pages), but they will send a free mini-catalog on request.

BEALL TOOL CO.

541 Swans Rd. NE   (800) 331-4718
Newark OH 43055   (614) 345-5045

The Beall wood threader for router use comes in three left-hand and five right-hand sizes. It is one of the tools I have not yet used, and one that I am itching to try. To add to my itch, Judith Beall sent along a copy of their *The Nuts & Bolts of Woodworking*, with twenty projects and a huge amount of information. Beall manufactures, distributes, and sells direct. Write or call for a very informative brochure.

BEAR WOODS SUPPLY CO.

Box 40, Dept. U   In Canada: (800) 565-5066
Bear River NS   (902) 467-3703
Canada B0S 1B0   FAX: (902) 467-3637

The unfinished wood items in Bear Woods free catalog include the only milk bottle and holder array I have seen, in addition to oodles of the usual, and hordes of the not-so-usual, wood parts. Other miniatures include books, hurricane lamps, bean pots, butter churns, bowling pins, bats, yo-yos, bells, needle boxes and thimbles, large bean pots and apple boxes, spindles of many kinds, towel bars and ball knobs, mushroom knobs and sidegrain knobs, cribbage pegs, checkers, dowel caps, spools, blocks, eggs and finials,

Bear Woods' milk bottle holder comes in two sizes, and there are many other shapes.

plus all the usual, and some unusual, wheels. The catalog is fun and prices are reasonable. Prospective U.S. customers had better check on currency conversions and shipping. For Canadians, shipping is free.

Bear Woods' spindle top array.

Bear Woods' knob array.

EDWARD J. BENNETT COMPANY

Fair Oaks Industrial Park
1016 Morse Ave.
Suite 21   (800) 333-4994
Sunnyvale CA 94089   (408) 744-0179

The TS-Aligner for table saws is a dial alignment gauge that will rapidly show whether or not the blade is parallel to the rip fence. Call or write for further information.

BEREA HARDWOODS COMPANY

125 Jacqueline Dr.
Berea OH 44017   (216) 243-4452

Berea offers exotic woods and unusual and figured domestic woods, with turning blocks and squares in burls, spalted, and other figures. Call or write for prices.

BILL BARTZ MANUFACTURING COMPANY

854 Arbor Oaks Dr.   (707) 451-9104
Vacaville CA 95687   (707) 451-4666

Bill's MitreRite costs $19.95 plus $3.00 shipping, and it works. It's a simple device — a series of devices, really — of plastic, including a tool for making four-sided frames, another for making six-sided frames, and a third that works for eight-sided frames, circles, and ovals. In essence, it is a flip-over guide that fits in front of the miter gauge on a table saw (with a minor procedure change, it works with radial arm saws too). The only requirement for table saws is that the miter gauge slots be parallel to the saw blade, which is a standard setup need in any case. The MitreRite then produces complementary angles, so that you have a good fit. One cut is made, the miter gauge and guide moved to the other gauge slot, and the second cut is made after flipping the guide over. Any deviation from an accurately angled cut is made up for when the gauge is moved and the guide flipped, so you get gap-free joints. The MitreRite won the Retailer's Choice Award at the National Hardware Show in August of 1992.

BJORN INDUSTRIES, INC.

551 King Edward
Charlotte NC 28211

Write for information on their eleven types of hide glue.

BLUE RIDGE MACHINERY & TOOLS, INC.

Box 536
Hurricane WV 25526   (304) 562-3538

The Blue Ridge Machinery catalog of power and hand tools is $1.00.

BLUME SUPPLY, INC.

3316 South Blvd.   (800) 288-9200
Charlotte NC 28209   (704) 523-7811

Powermatic and other power tools, sales, repair, and rental. In addition, they list everything from angle finders to hand saws to rules, squares, utility knives, wrenches — under hand tools. Blume also handles supplies for woodworkers, including wood buttons, plugs and dowels, glues, and screws. Call for prices, and other details.

BOULTER PLYWOOD CORP.

24 Broadway
Somerville MA 02145   (617) 666-1340

As the name leads you to believe, the emphasis at Boulter Plywood is on plywood. The free catalog shows Baltic birch and Chilean beech, both void-free types (that is, internal plies are laid up so that there are no gaps or holes inside the face and back plies). Boulter provides the specs and has their hardwood plywood made to fit. Various cuts are available, with plain and rotary slicing being the most common, though some of the oaks are rift sliced and one type of teak is quarter sawn. Face plies available include birch, cherry, mahogany, oak, walnut, pine, maple (plus curly and bird's eye), teak, rosewood, sapelli, okoume, hickory, and butternut. Edge banding veneers for all are available. Italian poplar is offered for its great flexibility, and the list of solid lumbers includes all the preceding, plus meranti, bubinga, goncalo alves, mansonia, padauk, purple heart, zebrawood, black limba, tigerwood, wenge, pippy elm, and pippy white oak. To round out their list, Boulter offers MDO, composition panels (flakeboard), lauan, aircraft plywood, and others. Well worth a look.

BRANDMARK BY

F&K Concepts
462 Carthage Dr.   (800) 323-2570
Beavercreek OH 45434-5865   (513) 426-6843

The project branding iron produced by F&K Concepts, called BrandMark, is available in several styles. The simplest is the type heated with a torch or hot plate. It costs $28.00. The electric branding iron is more complex, and costs $48.00. Either iron gives you a chance to quickly and permanently mark all your completed projects. The standard first line says: Handcrafted By. The second line can have up to twenty spaces, with a ¼" letter height. The first line can be changed, and third and fourth lines, and special figures, may all be added at extra cost.

BRIDGE CITY TOOL WORKS

1104 N.E. 28th St.
Suite 200
Portland OR 97232   (800) 253-3332

Bridge City Tool Works presents some of the most attractive hand measuring tools being made today, with most made of rosewood and brass (where appropriate). The $1.00 catalog will provide much more information and more than a couple of minutes time looking over true beauty.

BRISTOL VALLEY HARDWOODS

4300 Bristol Valley Rd.
Canandaigua NY 14424   (800) 724-0132

Bristol Valley stocks fish tail oak, padauk, wenge, lacewood, zebra, hickory, mahogany, pines, poplar, butternut, walnut, cherry, birch, white and red oak, and a great many others. The current catalog price list is $1.00.

BROOKSTONE

5 Vose Farm Rd.   Customer service: (800) 846-3000
Peterborough NH 03458   FAX: (603) 924-0093

For a long time now, Brookstone has provided odd and interesting items. Their catalog is called "Hard To Find Tools," but actually these days seems to cover more of a hard-to-find anything or odd items of interest to people who may or may not be so odd. A few things are of direct value to woodworkers, while others require either great imagination or a twisted mind to be classed as woodworking items. I like the catalog, and have found the products I ordered to be as represented. The catalog's list price is $3.00, but I have never paid for one, so call it free. I suggest you call and see if they will add you to their mailing list.

LARRY & FAYE BRUSSO COMPANY

3812 Cass-Elizabeth
Waterford MI 48328   (313) 682-4320

The Brussos produce exceptionally fine solid brass hardware for custom cabinetry and fine boxes. All hardware is machined from solid brass stock, hand fitted, and finished nicely, to produce show quality hinges. I have recently built a walnut hope chest using their hinges and find them truly exceptional. I suggest checking prices directly, because brass stock is fluctuating at press time. Brusso hinges are sold by many of the mail order firms and are available directly, in quantities of ten and up. Call or write for a retail price schedule.

CALCULATED INDUSTRIES

22720 Savi Ranch   (800) 854-8075
Yorba Linda CA 92687   (714) 921-1800
                    FAX: (714) 921-2799

The Construction Master II feet-inch calculator adds, subtracts, and divides in feet and inches, and with any fraction, from ½ to 1/64, including mixed fractions. The CMII will also convert between feet-inch fractions, decimal feet, inches, yards and metrics, including square and cubic measurements. With all of this, the CMII also works as a standard math calculator, with many functions, including square roots and auto shut-off. The company distributes and sells direct and accepts credit cards.

CAPE FORGE

P.O. Box 987
Burlington VT 05402

This small company success story is unusual in that the Cape Forge is a father and ... but not father and son. Mike De

Punte has as apprentice his daughter Karyn, who has a B.A. in Industrial Education and Technology. Karyn turns the hardwood handles for the tools, and attends to the fit and finish. Mike forges the blades. From the photos Karyn sent, the tools are obviously beautifully made. Most of their tools are for carvers and sculptors, but they do make paring chisels that I can hope to get, in at least one or two sizes, in the future. The catalog is $1.00.

CASCADE TOOLS, INC.

P.O. Box 3110
Bellingham WA 98227   (800) 235-0272

Cascade Tools imports and distributes the SY line of carbide tools, primarily router bits and shaper cutters. There are many unusual items in both arrays, plus such items as anti-kickback devices, knife-setting jigs, rub collars, dust collection connectors, router bases, roller brackets, and more, including books and videos, and air nailers (brad models) and staplers. The catalog is free and the 800 number takes orders twenty-four hours a day.

A Cascade Tools' cutter.

CATSKILL MOUNTAIN LUMBER COMPANY

P.O. Box 450
Swan Lake NY 12783   (800) 828-9663

The free catalog from Catskill Mountain Lumber presents paneling, flooring, white pine, and hardwoods direct from the sawmill. Measurement is done after drying, with hardwoods offered in "Select & Better," which combines the top three grades of the National Hardwood Lumber Association. Number 1 Common presents shorter, narrower lengths, with less clear lumber. All lumber is dried to a moisture content of 6% to 8%, furniture industry standard. Catskill Mountain Lumber offers ash, basswood, beech, hard maple, cherry, birch, red maple, red oak, yellow poplar, white oak, and Eastern white pine. Prices appear well within the normal range for this date and time, possibly a few cents to the lower side. In addition to lumber, CTL presents an array of router bits and some other tools, plus an interesting looking group of educational videos on the lumber industry, machinery, and other aspects of manufacturing wood.

CERTAINLY WOOD

11753 Big Tree Rd. E.   (716) 655-0206
Aurora NY 14052   FAX: (716) 655-3446

The free catalog shows fine veneers, in which Certainly Wood specializes, although they also offer lumber in twenty to thirty species. The fold-out, brochure-style catalog is exceptionally well done and shows a number of unusual woods in full color (Bee's Wing Eucalyptus, Eucalyptus burl, Quilted maple, Silkwood, etc.), and gives a short treatise on different figures such as Bird's Eye, Fiddleback, Curly, Mottled, Bee's Wing, and onward, each illustrated in full color. Available veneers include Bee's Wing Andiroba, Bubbly maple, Cat's Paw cherry (this is a new one on me, but it is said to have tiny burls that look like cat's pawprints), gnarly white oak, tiger bog oak, quilted moabi, imbuya burl, grafted walnut, redwood burls, olive ash burls. I counted seventy-three woods available in full-length veneers, with admittedly some being variations on one species — claro walnut, figured walnut, quartered white oak, rift white oak, flat sawn white oak. Prices appear to be well in line, and the extra information is worthwhile.

CHARLOTTE FORD TRUNKS

Box 536
Spearman TX 79081   (800) 659-3027

The catalog is $3.00 and features trunk building and repair parts, supplies, and books.

CHERRY TREE TOYS, INC.

P.O. Box 369
Belmont OH 43718   (800) 848-4363

Cherry Tree Toys may be most notable for the variety and quality of the shaped wood parts it carries, but it also has a good line of accessories, including drill bits, circle cutters, and even Sakura scroll saws, all at competitive prices. Cherry Tree also carries almost four dozen music box movements, with songs from "Amazing Grace" to "You Light Up My Life." There are also bank slot melody movements, mobile holder musical movements, blinking nose movements, touch movements, and others. The Cherry Tree line of kits includes a Conestoga wagon, a stagecoach, a chuckwagon, and hardware packages for a variety of other plans. There are many door harp plans too, and parts for those plans, and kits for door harps, plus cradle, doll house, and toy plans. Cherry Tree offers a line of solid brass stencils for letters and patterns that I have seen nowhere else. The Cherry Tree Toys catalog is $1.00 and is a must have for toy builders.

CLARK NATIONAL PRODUCTS, INC.

984 Amelia Ave.
San Dimas CA 91773   (714) 592-2016

Call or write for information on the Zyliss clamp.

CLARK CRAFT

16 Aqua Lane   (716) 873-2640
Tonawanda NY 14150   FAX: (716) 873-2651

Clark Craft presents a catalog of boat kits and plans, for a non-refundable $5.00, first class mail; $2.50 for bulk mail. The catalog order includes a separate boatbuilding supply catalog that includes books, more plans, many laminating and finishing tools and supplies, boat nails and screws (silicon bronze is the featured material), fiberglass cloth, matt, woven roving and tape, plus resins, with detailed instructions for the use of epoxy. The boat plan and kit catalog takes you from a canoe and a six-foot dinghy on up to a Roberts 64 sailboat. Along the way, there are plans for kayaks, hovercraft, tunnel hull runabouts, racers, house-boats, and even a 70' steel hull cruiser. Plans and pattern prices start as low as $20, and go up to $695 for the 70 steel hull cruiser, jumping to $749 for the Roberts 64. Study prints are available at far lower cost ($30 for the Roberts 64, $20 for the steel 70 footer). Boat kits start at $225 for the little dinghy, and scamper up to $6,650 for a Crown Cruiser 26'. Larger boats, and many not so large, are available only as plans kits, but some have frame, hull, and fastening kits available too.

CMT

5425 Beaumont Center Blvd.   U.S.: (800) 531-5559
Tampa FL 33634   Canada: (800) 387-7005

Premium router bits are featured in CMT's free catalog. Sets are available for Incra, JoinTech, Leigh, OmniJig, and Keller jigs. Call for the catalog.

COLONIAL HARDWOODS, INC.

7648 Dynatech Court   (800) 466-5451
Springfield VA 22153   FAX: (703) 451-0186

With over a hundred species in stock, Colonial Hardwoods should have what you need. They also stock burls for woodturners. Call for prices and a list of woods.

COLT CLAMP COMPANY, INC.

33 Swan St.   (800) 536-8420
Batavia NY 14020-3245   (716) 343-8622
                               FAX: (716) 343-8622

Call, fax, or write for a free catalog of a dozen eccentric clamp styles in aluminum, steel, and stainless steel.

CONOVER

Lathe Division
American Woodcraft Tools, Inc.   (800) 722-5447
10420 Kinsman Rd.   (216) 564-9600
Newbury OH 44065   FAX: (216) 564-9566

The Conover lathes are justly famous, using as a base a 16" bed design and partial or full kits to produce a lathe with an unlimited length. Call for a free catalog.

CONSTANTINE'S

2050 Eastchester Rd.
Bronx NY 10461   (800) 223-8087

Constantine's has been in business since 1812, in one form or another (not always mail order, and today, not totally mail order with two retail outlets). Almost any aspect of woodworking, with an emphasis on veneers, is to be found in the full-color catalog. Send $1.00 and go on the catalog list for two years. Constantine's carries many books, videos, and unusual finishing supplies, including their own line of water-based finishes, Micro-Mesh abrasive cloth, flocking, basswood plates, picture-framing materials, hardware, weaving materials and tools, and more.

CRAFT SUPPLIES USA

1287 E. 1120 S.
Provo UT 84606   (801) 373-0917

This wide line woodturning supplier offers a 48-page catalog of items from Woodfast (lathes), Henry Taylor and Sorby turning tools, and Dale Nish workshops. Catalog price is $2.00, refunded with order.

CRAFTSMAN WOOD SERVICE COMPANY

1735 W. Cortland Court   Orders only: (800) 543-9367
Addison IL 60101   Information: (708) 629-3100

For over sixty years, Craftsman Wood Service has been supplying veneers, hardware, other woodworking supplies, and many tools, in their $2.00 132-page catalog. Tools include the Dremel scroll saw line, plus the Moto-Tool and their flex-shaft tool, Jorgenson, Pony, and Quick-Grip clamps, Vix bits, and many veneering tools. Veneers carried are amaranth, zebra, vermilion, rosewood, coco bolo, bubinga, cherry, birch, gum, koa, mahogany, maple, oak, avodire, basswood, primavera, spruce, teak, walnut, and myrtle. Craftsman also sells turning squares, cabinet grade oak, cherry, walnut, and mahogany, balsa, red cedar, and poplar, among other woods.

CRAFTSMAN'S MART

P.O. Box 2342
Greeley CO 80631

Free bulk mail delivery of their 72-page catalog, or a $1.00 charge for first class mail delivery. Projects, parts, and supplies are covered, including over 350 varieties of Twinkle Tones, Touch-N-Play, bank slots, and other musical items.

CROWN CITY HARDWARE

1047 N. Allen Ave.
Pasadena CA 91104

For their handcrafted reproduction hardware catalog, Crown City asks $25.00. I would want to hear more about it before ordering, though it is said to list over a thousand items pictured at actual sizes in its 200 pages, along with a brief history of many European styles.

CUSTOM WOOD CUT-OUTS UNLIMITED

P.O. Box 518
Massillon OH 44648

The catalog is $2.00, refundable with your first order. Not only does Custom Wood Cut-Outs make all the scrolled wood cut-outs in their catalog, they will also live up to their name and produce custom cuts from your drawing. Check with them for quantities and prices. Cut-outs range from smaller than a tiny pumpkin (1¾" x 1¼") on up to bird houses and feeders, toy wagons, shadow boxes in three sizes and styles, and a sled. Prices range from $.29 for the pumpkin to $30.25 for a thirteen-piece Nativity set. The catalog shows almost six hundred cut-outs, plus Shaker pegs, wheels, and paints.

D.F. ENTERPRISES

27 Wills Rd.   (412) 626-8870
Connellsville PA 15425   FAX: (412) 626-8872

Call to check on the $3.00 catalog of drawers and cabinet fronts.

DELTA TECHNICAL COATINGS, INC.

2550 Pellissier Place   (800) 423-4135
Whittier CA 90601   In CA: (800) 553-8940
                                    (213) 686-0678

Hallmark Home Decor Antiquing Gel is one of Delta's Home Decor line of water-based stains and finishes. Gel wood stain, liquid wood stain, pickling gel, antiquing gel, neutral gel, transparent pearl glaze gel, gel stain retarder, and an acrylic paint base coat make up most of the line. To make it possible to go from the wood out with the same compatible product line, Home Decor products include wood sealer; dimensional stain resist (used to mask areas to be left unstained); water-based interior varnish in matte, satin, and gloss; an exterior gloss varnish; and wood filler. Products are generally available in two- and eight-ounce containers. Give them a call and request details.

DEROSE & COMPANY

Box 150   (804) 746-1705
Mechanicsville VA 23111   FAX: (804) 746-2556

This manufacturer of custom lathes offers features that will make a woodturner's mouth water or hands try to grasp the nearest turning tool. The basic unit has a swing of 25" or 30", with a sliding, rotating head stock (rotation is for outboard turning). The distance between centers can range from 42" (or less) to 102", which is more than sufficient for general use, including bed post turning, unless you have to have a bed post longer than 8½'. Information on the DeRose lathe and its options, including lengths greater than 102", can be had for a phone call or a card.

DISCOUNT ARTS AND CRAFTS WAREHOUSE

9015 US 19 North
Pinellas Park FL 34666

Discount Arts and Crafts offers a free flyer or a 236-page catalog for $2.00.

DONJER PRODUCTS

Ilene Court
Bldg. 8
Bellemead NJ 08502   (800) 336-6537

Call or write for DonJer's free brochure explaining their spray-on suede.

DOYEL ENTERPRISES

P.O. Box 315
Yorba Linda CA 92686-0315   (714) 666-1770

Doyel makes and sells a miter fence system for radial arm saws. The system is said to eliminate the multiple grooves all over the saw table and to provide accuracy to within ¼ degree. Call or write for information.

DUNLAP WOODCRAFTS

Wolf Trap Run Rd.
Vienna VA 22182   (703) 631-5147

This producer of Appalachian hardwoods offers curly maple and other fine woods, plus a normal run of maple, oaks, walnut, and cherry. Call to check prices on what you need.

EAGLE AMERICA CORPORATION

P.O. Box 1099
Chardon OH 44024   (800) 872-2511

The Eagle router bit catalog is free and has 64 pages covering large selections of American-made bits, with upwards of six hundred new items.

EBAC LUMBER DRYERS

106 John Jefferson Rd.   (800) 433-9011
Suite 102   (804) 229-3038
Williamsburg VA 23185   FAX: (804) 229-3321

For the heavy wood user, Ebac presents three lumber dryer systems that sell for under $3,000, with systems perfected to the point where no experience is needed to get perfectly dried lumber. An example is the TR250, which works on loads from 50 to 250 board feet, drying lumber to 6 to 8% moisture content (recommended cabinet-making range). The buyer builds the kiln chamber, which is one reason the price is within reason. Call or write for further information.

ECON-ABRASIVES

P.O. Box 865021
Plano TX 75086   (214) 377-9779

Emphasizing low cost, Econ-Abrasives does present good prices on sanding belts and other tools. The catalog is free.

EDMUND SCIENTIFIC

101 E. Gloucester
Pike Barrington NJ 08007   (609) 573-6260

The free catalog from Edmund Scientific offers varied parts that are not woodworking materials or tools, but that often are useful in setting up jigs or preparing projects.

ELECTROPHYSICS

Box 1143, Station B
London ONT
Canada N6A 5K2   (519) 668-2871

Eight models of wood moisture meters for home or industrial uses. Call or write for free catalog.

EMPEROR CLOCK COMPANY

Emperor Industrial Park
Fairhope AL 36532   (205) 928-2316

Emperor's clock kits and furniture kits come in solid oak and cherry and let you furnish your home at a fraction of the cost of already built furniture, before you develop all the skills required for full-scale, complex woodworking. All parts are pre-cut, and the frames and doors have already been assembled. For those who are undecided on woodworking as a pastime, these kits may provide the deciding factor. The color catalog is $1.00.

EUREKA HARDWOOD SUPPLY

3346 D St.
Eureka CA 95501   (707) 445-3371

The price list is free, but owner Guy Helmuth recommends you give him a call to check on availability of burl and figured western species after you get the list. Eureka Hardwood also mails a postcard bulletin about once a month listing discoveries; you may ask to be placed on this list. The current list contains burls of buckeye, madrone, manzanita, maple, myrtle, California nutmeg, redwood bird's eye, redwood root, California walnut, Douglas fir, and holly half-logs (cants). Other woods listed include English walnut grafts on Claro, with the graft close to the center of the blank, English walnut, Pacific yew, figured Monterey cypress, Port Orford cedar (burls and said to be rare), and redwood bunion burls. Odd logs and half logs in almond, apple, black acacia, olive, plum, yew, and curly maple are also available. Guy also sells straight lumber in many of the above species, plus golden chinkapin, Oregon ash, Oregon white oak, tan oak, sugar pine, Western quilted maple, and Pacific dogwood. All in all, an exceptionally interesting list, with a 100% guarantee of satisfaction.

EXCALIBUR

210 Eighth St. S.
Lewiston NY 14092   (800) 387-9789

The Excalibur T slot saw fence, with its various accessories, is a reasonably easy to install replacement and upgrade unit for table saws. I used one for years on my Delta Unisaw, and found it met every claim made for it. Accessories include a router table to be built into the saw fence extension table, router fence brackets, a stock pusher, and guide rail work stops. Two stock guide rail lengths are available, allowing rip cuts to the right of the blade of 33" and 62"; and two fence lengths, for different size saw tables, are available. Excalibur makes its own sliding table for table saws, allowing excellent crosscut accuracy to go with the T-slot fence's great rip cut accuracy. For those who have not used them, sliding tables on stationary saws add fantastic cutting abilities and accuracy, if well made. The Excalibur comes in two sizes, the EXSLT30, giving a 28" crosscut depth (to the front of a 10" blade), and the EXSLT60, with a crosscut depth of 37". Excalibur also offers an over-arm blade cover for dust collection. More information is available from Excalibur, and the units are available from them directly, as well as from other retailers.

EXOTIC HARDWOODS

4100 Spencer St.
Torrance CA 90503   (213) 542-3576

Write for their free catalog of hardwoods.

FEIN POWER TOOLS, INC.

3019 West Carson St.
Pittsburgh PA 15204   (800) 441-9878

Call for information on Fein's triangular pad sander for corner work and similar tight spots.

FRAMEWEALTH

RD 2, Box 261-7
Otego NY 13825   (800) 524-8582

For those whose interest is in framing pictures or other items, FrameWealth presents a goodly number of framers' moldings, both as ready-mades and as parts. Framers' tools and hardware, from a miter vise to picture wire, are listed. The catalog is free.

FRANK MITTERMEIER, INC.

P.O. Box 2
3577 E. Tremont
Bronx NY 10465   (212) 828-3843

An importer of woodworking tools, Mittermeier presents a free catalog that shows, among other things, a line of Forstner bits.

FREEBORN TOOL COMPANY, INC.

6202 North Freya
P.O. Box 6246   (800) 523-8988
Spokane WA 99207-0904   FAX: (509) 484-9932

Panel cutters are Freeborn's forte — all they make and all they want to make. The line is wide, and interesting, if you use a shaper. Cutters are tipped with Tantung, a name that brought a fast "Whaaa?" from me. Essentially, Tantung is an alloy of cobalt, chromium, tungsten, columbium, and carbon. Heat resistance is far higher than that of high speed steel, and the resistance to shock is higher than that of carbide, though Tantung will not take as much heat as carbide. Tantung is not intended for use on manmade fiber and plywood materials. Freeborn's range of cutters includes all the usual, such as lock miter and single tongue and groove lock miter sets, drawer lock cutters, drop leaf table cutters, and so on. Freeborn also makes custom cutters, so if there is a shaper profile you need and can't find, this company will work with you. Check the catalog and their brochures first because there is a plethora of stock shapes.

G & W TOOL CO., INC.

P.O. Box 691464
Tulsa OK 74169   (918) 486-2761

Free literature describes the Wagner Safe-T-Planer, an accessory that fits radial arm saws and drill presses. The planers are made of die cast aluminum and high speed steel that is precision ground. Basically, the tools turn a drill press or radial arm saw into a planer, allowing you to cut molding patterns, raised panels, tapered legs, rabbets, tenons, and similar patterns. The tool cannot kick back and is low cost. G & W Tool Co. sells directly, and the Wagner Safe-T-Planer is also available from most mail order houses.

GARRETT WADE COMPANY

161 Ave. of the Americas
New York NY 10013-1299   (800) 221-2942

The lush regular catalog is $4.00 and shows about as wide a variety of hand tools and power tool accessories as it is practical to offer. Certainly there is the widest array of chisels of any company including their top-of-the-line house brand, Marples, Robert Sorby, Bacho Ergo, Iyoroi, Stubai, Shokunin, and others, often in hard-to-find styles and sizes, including swan neck models, several corner chisels, Sorby's Registered Mortise chisels, dog-leg, and other styles. The catalog is replete with color and with tips on tool use. It may have the highest "drool" factor of any tool catalog because of the excellent photography and layout and the number and variety of tools presented. Garrett Wade offers two other catalogs, one on brass hardware and one for master craftsmen. The Master Craftsman catalog is an update of the annual and offers specific and unusual items, some of which may not be found elsewhere. For example, I have seen Sorby's special tools for ring cutting only one other place. These six tools make the turning of captive rings (rings turned on a shaft and trapped inside end pieces) easy for most lathe workers. The process is normally very demanding, requiring a lot of practice. If you have an unusual need not met by any other tool supplier, check out the Garrett

Wade catalogs. The articles on turning tools and tool sharpening are almost worth the catalog cost. No place is a one-stop source for a woodworker's every need (if it were, there would be no need for this book), but Garrett Wade fills many needs, from Hydrocote finishes to dozens of books, to bow saw kits, to Japanese tools.

GENEVA SPECIALTIES

P.O. Box 542
Lake Geneva WI 53147   (800) 556-2548

Call for their free catalog of plans, wood parts, and hardware.

GIL-LIFT

1605 North River
Independence MO 64050   (816) 833-0611

For those of us who from time to time build wall-mounting cabinets, this lift for cabinet installation seems to be an ideal solution to a pernicious problem (getting the cabinet to stay in place, without a helper and without a massive framework of aids, while attaching it to the wall). Gil Wyand makes only this one tool, and will send free information on request.

GILLIOM MANUFACTURING, INC.

P.O. Box 1018
St. Charles MO 63302   (314) 724-1812

If you have any desire to make your own power tools, kits from Gilliom may be the incentive you need to get started. The list includes a 12" bandsaw, an 18" bandsaw; a 10" tilt arbor table saw, a lathe and drill press combination, a 9" tilt-table table saw, a 6" belt sander, a spindle shaper, and a circular saw table, at $7.50 each or $25.00 for the package of eight plans. Gilliom also manufactures kits to help you in building the tools. The descriptive brochure is $2.00.

GILMER WOOD CO.

2211 NW St. Helens Rd.
Portland OR 97210   (503) 274-1271

Gilmer Wood features a very large inventory with a few woods I have never heard of before, at least in a woodworking context. Availability ranges from logs to blanks, and includes burls, slabs from 1" to 6" thick, paneling, and plain old-fashioned boards. The Gilmer Wood catalog is un-illustrated, $2.00, and has to be worth it to anyone looking for boxwood, African blackwood, aniegre, burl amboyna, alerce, Alaskan yellow cedar, cocuswood, damar minyak, imbuya, jelutong, koto, makore, and numerous other exotics, plus domestic hardwoods of almost all kinds. Ask also about lists of woods for cutlery handles, instruments, and sculpture.

GOBY'S WALNUT WOOD PRODUCTS

5016 Palestine Rd.
Albany OR 97321   (503) 926-7516

Oregon walnut is a gorgeous wood: the photos Gary Goby sent me are of highly figured pieces and in color, which means we can't show them here. The free Goby's price list covers 4/4 through 16/4 stock in Number 1&2 Commons through FAS (Firsts and Seconds) and on to Clears at reasonable prices. Current mill run is $2.50 a board foot (4/4 to 5/4 material; thicker is higher), plus shipping, a low price for walnut. All lumber is 6" or wider, and other shapes and thicknesses are available, including rough cut gun stock blanks and turning stock. A list of specials is sent as they become available. The current one shows much Oregon black walnut, but includes fir and Oregon white oak.

GRANBERG INTERNATIONAL

P.O. Box 425
Richmond CA 94807   (510) 237-2099

Granberg makes a chainsaw lumber mill that appears similar to one I used about twenty years ago. I believe the company thought it mailed more to me than it did (two photos and an empty envelope), but the mill is an attachment for your own chainsaw, and is thus about the most economical kind of small sawmill you can find. The wide kerf chainsaw cut wastes more wood than do bandsaw and circular saw mills, and chainsaw mills are more time consuming to use, but the start-up cost is a small fraction of the cost of either of those types. Drop a line to the company to check out specifications and prices.

GREAT LAKES LEATHER PRODUCTS CO.

4022 North 45th St.
Sheboygan WI 53083   (414) 458-8489

Write or call for free literature on woodworker's leather aprons. Two designs are currently offered, with line expansion in the works. One is a classic leather apron; the other is a farrier's (horseshoer's) leather apron, with upper leg protection.

GRIZZLY IMPORTS, INC.

West of the Mississippi:
P.O. Box 2069
Bellingham WA 98227-2069   (800) 541-5537
East of the Mississippi:
2406 Reach Rd.
Williamsport PA 17701   (800) 523-4777

The Grizzly catalog, a sizable book (about 140 color pages) is free from either location, both of which are showroom and warehouse locations. Grizzly is a major importer of Taiwanese stationary tools, but no longer stops there. Their catalog shows the expected lines of table saws, planers, dust collectors, sanders, jointers, bandsaws, and more. Added to that is Grizzly's line of accessories of many kinds, from sanding belts and abrasive discs to mortising attachments and chisels, plus their own line of framing and brad nailers and staplers. In addition, they carry Makita tools and Campbell-Hausfeld air compressors and accessories, plus a reasonable line of books and videos. Add to that a short but handy line of European cabinet hardware and more, and the catalog becomes very interesting.

GROFF & HEARNE LUMBER

858 Scotland Rd.	(800) 342-0001
Quarryville PA 17566	(717) 284-0001

Groff & Hearne supplies curly cherry and many other fine woods up to 40" wide, specializing in walnut and cherry. They use a bandsaw mill, and air dry lumber slowly before sending it to finish out in the kiln. Lumber is sold rough or dressed, as you prefer, there is no minimum order, and orders may be shipped UPS or common carrier (truck). Groff & Hearne features domestic lumber, including walnut, cherry, red oak, white oak, ash, birch and flame birch, poplar, Honduras mahogany, sassafras, hard maple, tiger maple, bird's eye maple, with a few exotics such as coco bolo, padauk, purpleheart, zebrawood, and back to the more usual English walnut, butternut, Eastern white pine, apple, and chestnut. (I don't know where they get the chestnut, but will shortly check prices on that. I would like to make a small box or two.) Their price list is free.

HARTWOOD, LTD.

P.O. Box 397
New Oxford PA 17350   (717) 624-9292

Appalachian and exotic hardwoods are featured in the list Hartwood will send you for a self-addressed stamped envelope. They also carry veneers and plywoods, turning and carving blocks, Freud products, and West system epoxies.

HIDA TOOL, INC./GYOKUCHO JAPAN

1333 San Pablo Ave.
Berkeley CA 94702   (800) 443-5512

For a free brochure on Japanese saws, drop Hida Tool a line. For a full catalog, send $3.00.

HIGHLAND HARDWARE

1045 N. Highland Ave. NE
Atlanta GA 30306   (800) 872-4466

Highland Hardware presents one of the more complete woodworking accessories and tools catalogs. It is free for a call to their 800 number or a note to their address. Brands include all major names, and move on to some — such as EagleSpray, in the HVLP field — that may not be familiar to the average woodworker. A very well-done catalog with extensive informational material in the form of actual articles in each issue. The list of tools includes some super new ones that I had yet to hear a word about, so they do keep their catalog updated well. Prices seem comparable to those of other mail order houses.

HILLSIDE WOODCRAFT

920 Center Church Rd.
East Earl PA 17519   (215) 445-7287

Call or write for information on cedar chest kits.

HOME LUMBER CO.

449 Whitewater St.
Whitewater WI 53190   (800) 262-5482

Call or write for listings of tools and woodworking supplies.

HORTON BRASSES

Nooks Hill Rd.
P.O. Box 120
Cromwell CT 06416   (203) 635-4400

The Horton catalog of reproduction furniture hardware is $3.00.

INDUSTRIAL ABRASIVES CO.

643 N. 8th St.	(800) 428-2222
Reading PA 19612	In PA: (800) 222-2292

Industrial Abrasives offers sanding belts and similar tools, showcasing them in their free catalog.

INTERNATIONAL TOOL CORPORATION

1939 Tyler St.	(800) 338-3384
Hollywood FL 33020	FAX: (305) 927-0291

International Tools is a full line distributor of quality industrial power tools, featuring Porter-Cable, Bosch, Milwaukee, Hitachi, Skil, Ryobi, Delta, Panasonic, Freud, Senco, Stanley-Bostitch, and many more. Eighty-page catalog is free.

JAMESTOWN DISTRIBUTORS

28 Narragansett Ave.	(800) 423-0030
P.O. Box 348	(401) 423-2520
Jamestown RI 02835	FAX: (401) 423-0542

If you're looking for a wide range of fasteners and other boatbuilding and woodworking supplies, the Jamestown catalog's 200 pages (free on request) will cover those needs. The fastener section starts with 18-8 stainless steel wood screws, goes on through machine screws, nuts and bolts, cotter pins, cap screws, and washers, then swings into silicon bronze fasteners, and rivets in stainless steel, aluminum, and carbon steel. Nails are copper, brass, stainless steel, silicon bronze, and galvanized. Jamestown also carries general cleanup, caulk, adhesive, and similar items, with a strong emphasis on the West System epoxies, probably the most complete woodworking epoxy line whether for marine or other purposes. There are complete materials for fiberglass lay-up and laminating. The catalog has a strong section on

marine finishes, and another on accessories such as saw blades, drill bits, and hammers. An interesting catalog.

JAPAN WOODWORKER

1731 Clement
Alameda CA 94501 (800) 537-7820

The lines of Japanese woodworking tools in this catalog (two-year subscription for $1.50) are extensive, and the company is the original importer of Japanese woodworking tools and a principal supplier today, both retail and wholesale. There are many top quality tools of American make in the catalog as well. You may find yourself selecting from Starrett (truly precise measuring tools, generally meant for machine shop use but great for woodworking uses as well), Lie-Nielsen, Veritas, Akafuji Kanna, Dai, Shizen, Sada-kuzura, Hock, Bridge City Tool Works, and Razorsaw. I have used only a few Japanese tools, enough to be impressed with their superb cutting characteristics, and uneasy about their social meaning: what does it say about a society when virtually all cutting tools are meant to be used while drawing toward the user? Still, the cuts are unbeatable, and I have never found anything that comes close to Japanese water

Porter-Cable's SandTrap dust removal systems fit their sanders.

stones for sharpening ease and results on almost any edged tool — knives, chisels, plane irons all benefit strongly from a two- or three-step process on the stones.

Japanese saws give superb results and do double duty, while also being very specialized: this is a ryoba, or a double-sided beginner's carpentry saw. Courtesy of Japan Woodworker.

Japanese edge beveling planes do a really nice job. Courtesy of Japan Woodworker.

Japanese planes work by drawing toward the woodworker. Courtesy of Japan Woodworker.

JOINTECH CORP.

P.O. Box 790727
San Antonio TX 78279

This is a positioning tool similar to the Incra jig. Write for free brochure and a dealer name.

BOB KAUNE

511 11th
Port Angeles WA 98362   (206) 452-2292

For a current antique and used tools list send $3.00. For a five list subscription, the cost is $10.00.

KESTREL TOOL

Route 1, Box 1762
Lopez WA 98261   (206) 468-2103

Handmade tools for sculptors and carvers. The Kestrel Tool catalog is $2.00.

KLEIN DESIGN INC.

17910 SE 110th St.
Renton WA 98059   (206) 226-5937

Klein Design produces two miniature lathes, one of which is a full pattern lathe with a 12" bed length. The other is a short bed model. In addition, many jigs and tools are available for the lathes (threading jigs, scroll chuck, custom jaws, indexing system, hole-drilling guides, and more). Videos on lathe use are also sold, with a series of five covering just about everything you wish to know about miniature turning, down to using unusual materials — horn, bone, cast polyester, mother of pearl, Corian, and others — to making turned boxes with threaded lids. Call or drop a note for the latest brochure and price lists.

KLINGSPOR ABRASIVES

P.O. Box 2367   (800) 645-5555
Hickory NC 28603   (704) 322-3030

Klingspor is an abrasives manufacturer that also sells its products by mail, which makes them ideal for inclusion in this book. Send or call for a free color catalog, which will vary in size and content according to sales, and similar requirements. Headquartered in Hickory, NC, Klingspor has recently expanded to Ventura, CA, to better serve that market. Products include belt and disc abrasives with a wide variety of coat styles (open and closed) added to different backing materials. Prices are reasonable to low, with quantity discounts.

KLOCKIT

P.O. Box 636
Lake Geneva WI 53147   (800) KLOCKIT

Mail order clock kits, movements, faces, and virtually all clock-making accessories. The Klockit emphasis is on quartz battery movements, including some moderately massive chiming pendulum and dual pendulum types (not as long or large as truly massive mechanical movements, with a maximum bob diameter of about 3½" on a 20" long pendulum). You will also find mechanicals, with cable driven movements, bobs over 10" in diameter, and a wide variety of grandfather and grandmother clock faces. Case kits, full kits, cuckoo clocks, fretwork project kits (available ready to cut or already laser cut), and music box kits with fifty-note movements. There is even a two-page spread of wristwatches, and a fair assortment of accessories such as brad point drill bits, sanding drums, Forstner bits, and wood and brass parts. Catalog is free.

KUEMPEL CHIME

21195 Minnetonka Blvd.
Excelsior MN 55331

Red-I-Cut clock kits and movements are listed in the free Kuempel catalog.

THE LAMP SHOP

P.O. Box 36
Concord NH 03302   (603) 224-1603

Lamp parts for woodworkers are featured in The Lamp Shop's $2.00 catalog (to which they add a 36-page lamp shade instruction book if you send $8.00).

LEICHTUNG WORKSHOPS

4944 Commerce Parkway   (800) 237-5907
Cleveland OH 44128   (216) 464-6764

Leichtung offers a variety of unusual tools, some woodworking supplies, and a free catalog. The catalog is digest size but runs over 90 pages, and presents joint-making jigs, some kits (varying with the seasons, but often small boxes and clocks), router bits, Lervad folding workbenches, and a multitude of small items, including possibly the widest variety of doweling jigs in any single catalog. Equi-Pressure glue-up clamps were first offered by Leichtung and present a major help in gluing up flat boards (that's experience speaking!). They are not perfect, but they're very good and fairly low cost compared to systems that come from other makers. The catalog has many other styles of clamps and is the only tool catalog

I have seen where you are as likely to find wildflower seeds (by the small sack), rain gauges, and cowhide gloves as you are Forstner drill bits. I have used a lot of Leichtung's gloves and always keep several pair on hand. For the price, they are the best I have seen for light chores, up to and including feeding a planer.

LEIGH INDUSTRIES, LTD.

P.O. Box 357	
1585 Broadway St.	(800) 663-8932
Port Coquitlam BC	(604) 464-2700
Canada V3C 4K6	FAX: (604) 464-7404

Leigh jigs offer an incredible variety of choices in joint-making, starting with dovetails. The basic jig offers the ability to cut almost every kind of dovetail, including through, half-blind, sliding, end-on-end, and more, in wood to 1¼" thick. There is a multiple mortise and tenon attachment and a vast array of cutters to assist you in doing what you wish to do. The catalog is free and beautifully done, and Leigh sells directly, as well as through distributors.

LIE-NIELSEN TOOLWORKS

Route 1
Warren ME 04684   (800) 327-2520

These makers of heirloom quality hand tools offer a free brochure. The tools are lovely, lovingly made, and should be used the same way. Tools may be bought through many retailers or directly.

LOBO POWER TOOLS

9034 Bermudez St.	Order line: (800) 786-5626
Pico Rivera CA 90660	(213) 949-3747
	Atlanta: (404) 416-6006

Lobo imports stationary power tools, including table saws, bandsaws, spindle shapers, jointers, and wide belt sanders. They offer a free brochure and a $3.00 catalog, and sell direct.

LRH ENTERPRISES, INC.

CO-ST Cutter Bits	
7101 Valjean Ave.	(800) 423-2544
Van Nuys CA 91406	(818) 782-0226

Shaper cutters from LRH in stock patterns appear to cover about any profile one is apt to want, and the company also does custom cutter production. The newest line is the CO-ST Cutters designed to fit ½" and ¾" spindle shapers (sizes more likely to be in the small shop than the larger units). Give them a call to request literature or information.

MAFELL NORTH AMERICA

80 Earheart Dr.	
Unit 9	(716) 626-9303
Williamsville NY 14221	(716) 626-9304

Mafell North America sells unusual German tools. Many are designed for timber framing use, including a two-man circular saw with a 25³⁄₁₆" blade. Their small circular saw takes blades 13¾" to 17¾" and cuts to 5³⁄₁₆" deep at a 45 degree angle! The little saw weighs 63 pounds, versus 116.6 pounds for its big brother. Mafell also imports the Erika push-pull table saw, which provides the benefits of both table and radial arm saw in one unit, with free blade operation allowing 11" of blade travel through the wood, and with a fixed blade operation similar to other ⅝" arbor, 10" to 12" blade diameter saws (the Erika takes an 11" blade, something of an oddity in this country). The Erika is light at 82 pounds, and takes a wide assortment of accessories and supports, including a sliding table, micro adjust rip fence attachment, and double cross and miter cut fence guide. Tools are pricey, as European woodworking tools tend to be, but offer features not found in U.S.-made units. Also offered are a shaper, a planer-thicknesser-jointer, a dust and chip collector, a plunge cut router, an orbital sander, a belt sander, a jig saw, and many timber framing tools such as chainsaw mortisers. Call or write for information. Erika catalog $1.00.

MASON & SULLIVAN

586 Higgins Crowell Rd.
W. Yarmouth
Cape Cod MA 02673

The Mason & Sullivan line includes antique reproduction clock kits and parts. The catalog is free. Mason & Sullivan is now part of Woodcraft.

MASTODON TOOL

P.O. Box 17506	
Portland OR 97217	(503) 283-6838

Jaw extenders fit standard ¾" pipe clamps and give an 8" deep reach, with swivel ends. Give a call or drop a note for further details.

MAURICE L. CONDON CO., INC.

242 Ferris Ave.	(914) 946-4111
White Plains NY 10603	FAX: (914) 946-3779

Condon's offers domestic and foreign hardwoods, custom millwork, mouldings, veneers, and more in afrormosia, anigre, ash, avodire, balsa, basswood, beech, birch, cherry, chestnut, cocobolo, cypress, greenheart, hickory, holly, laurel, lignum vitae, imbuya, koa, paldao, pearwood, padauk, ramin, redwood, sapele, sycamore, teak, and many others. Their 32-page color catalog is $2.00.

J. & D. MCCOMBIE

5273 Gertrude St.
Port Alberni, B.C.
Canada V9Y 6L1   (604) 723-3074

I've seen drawings and read descriptions of the "Original Jimmy Jig" soon to be made and sold (plans are now all that's sold), and it sounds delightful for working large panels. Plans are $25.00, and the cost estimate is $35.00 if construction is from ½" plywood. Weight is said to be about 20 pounds, and the allowable rip width is 53" to either the left or the right of the blade. (The table adapts easily for use to the left of the blade.) Jim McCombie is a custom cabinetmaker who designed the unit to fill what he believes is a real lack.

McFEELY'S

P.O. Box 3   (800) 443-7937
Lynchburg VA 24505   FAX: (804) 847-7136

For me, this is about as local as suppliers get, but the catalog is fascinating. If you want instruction in square drive screws, the McFeely catalog is the place to get it. Pages 3 to 5 are devoted to telling you everything from reasons for using square drive screws to screw size needs for particular types of work, and on to screw head styles, lengths to use, and how a screw is made. A page or two later, the McFeely's catalog presents Warrington hammers, master chuck keys, storage bins, rigger's bags, drill bits, gimlets, biscuit joiners, Incra systems, Apollo HVLP spray systems (these are not the relatively low-priced Campbell-Hausfeld and Wagner units, but full-scale industrial units, with the cheapest running about 2½ times the price of the Campbell-Hausfeld, which is the least costly of the two lower-priced units currently on the market), Behlen and Watco finishes, toymaker's parts, project books, and much else. The catalog is $1.00.

MIDWEST DOWEL WORKS

5631 Hutchinson Rd.
Cincinnati OH 45248   (513) 574-8488

Call or write the company for a free catalog showing and listing dowels, plugs, pegs, and other items.

MIRACLE POINT

P.O. Box 71
Crystal Lake IL 60014-0071   (815) 477-7713

Miracle Point has one product line — tweezers — and at a reasonable cost there is a version that specifically suits

woodworkers, so no catalog is sent. The Miracle Point Magna-Point is a sharp tweezers combined with a 5X magnifying glass. Cost is $9.95 plus $2.00 for shipping. They sent a sample, and I have just used them to remove a splinter. They work and seem to ease the job.

MLCS, LTD.

P.O. Box 4053 C13   (800) 533-9298
Rydal PA 19046   FAX: (215) 938-5070

The free MLCS catalog features router bits but also offers quite a few other items. The router bits are reputed to be top quality (I have never used any of this brand) and come in a wide variety of profiles, including raised panel, stile and rail, multiform molding makers, French provincial, double ogee and double flute raised panel bits, an ogee raised panel bit with an undercutter, crown molding bits, and a slew of other molding bits, plus standard cove and bead, chamfer, Roman ogee, round over, beading, drawer and finger pull, ogee fillet, and thumbnail bits. There are round nose bits, core box bits, keyhole cutting bits, dish cutters, spiral downcut bits, door lip bits, hinge mortising bits, straight bits, bottom cleaning bits, lock miter bits, finger joint bits, tongue and groove bits, flush trimming bits, and others. Other products include Forstner drill bits, from ¼" to 3⅛" in size, shaper cutters, their own router table, an adjustable corner clamp, and other items. The catalog is definitely worth looking at, the inventory is large, and there are experienced woodworkers on staff to help with questions.

MOON'S SAW & TOOL INC.

2531-39 Ashland Ave.   (800) 477-7371
Chicago IL 60614   (312) 549-7924
          FAX: (312) 549-7695

This Chicago company presents a quarterly sale brochure and a small general lines catalog, plus a catalog of Byrom router bits, free and on request. The catalog is good-sized and presents Bessey clamps, as well as Jorgensen, Pony, Quick-Grip, Tru-Grip, and others. Sandvik and Marples chisels are carried, as are Record Coronet lathes, Electro bandsaw blade brazers, many router accessories, JoinTech woodworking positioning machines, drill bits, table saw accessories, Seco dust collectors, and a great many other items. The catalog, small in overall size, carries some unusual items. Worth looking at, as is the sales brochure.

BOB MORGAN WOODWORKING
SUPPLIES, INC.

1123 Bardstown Rd.   (502) 456-2545
Louisville KY 40204   FAX: (502) 456-4752

Bob Morgan emphasizes veneers in his catalog but also sells a good variety of solid hardwoods, both domestic and imported, including spalted maple, bacote, mahogany, basswood, cocobolo, and poplar. Morgan is noted for packaging cut-offs at low prices, and he now sells ebony mill ends among such packages. Check the redwood burl slabs (up to 48" x 22"), maple burl slabs to the same size, zirocote mill ends, maple and redwood burl bowl blanks, lignum vitae mill ends and other woods. He also sells 1/16" curly and bird's eye maple veneers, lacewood in 3/4" thickness, and burled jewelry box faces, as well as oak raised panel cabinet doors. Veneers include maple, white and red oak, cherry, mahogany, tiger oak, walnut, curly maple, ribbon sapele, rosewood, pomele, padauk, zebra wood, teak, fiddleback anegre, African satinwood, African makore, Carpathian elm burl, olive ash burl, mahogany crotch, and a number of pressure-sensitive and pre-glued walnut and oak pieces. Small tools and hardware are spotted throughout the catalog as well.

MURRAY CLOCK CRAFT LTD.

510 McNicholl Ave.
Willowdale ONT
Canada M2H 2E1   (416) 499-4531

The 69-page catalog is $2.00, refundable on your first order.

Murray Clock Craft carries grandmother, grandfather, wall, and shelf clocks, with a wide range of plans and kits, movements, and dials, battery or weight or spring driven.

MUSICMAKER'S KITS, INC.

423 South Main   (800) 432-KITS
Stillwater MN 55082   (612) 439-9120

Jerry Brown seems to offer about every type of acoustic instrument kit that might be of interest. The kit list includes hammer dulcimers, mountain dulcimers, harps, banjos, guitars, mountain mandolins, steel string guitar (six- or twelve-string), an item called a hurdy-gurdy, string bass, panpipes, wooden fife, garden harp, window harp, door harps, wooden drum, thumb piano, full-sized harps, and a series of special order kits that include a Martin classical guitar, a violin, a small bagpipe, and even a spinet harpsichord. In addition, Jerry has bits and pieces for scratch builders, including tuning pins, fret scale graph, eyelets, and much more. To work from plans, get one of his door harp or guitar plans, or any of a couple dozen other plans for everything from a hammer dulcimer to a psaltery. (Actually, from a banjo to a violin, if we stay alphabetical.) Woods, dyes, finishes, and clamps are also offered.

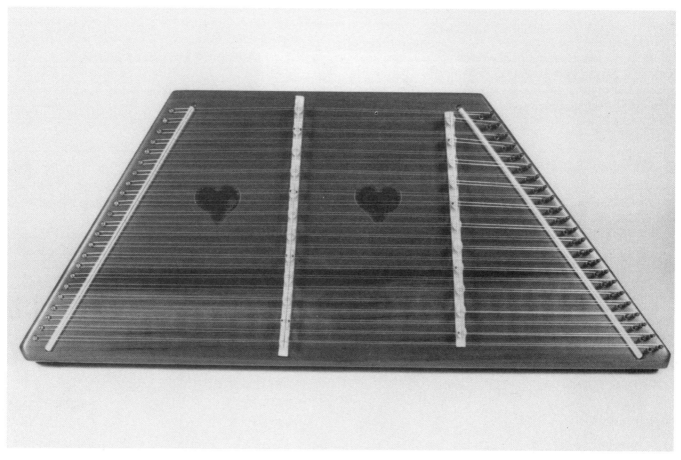

A redwood hammer dulcimer. Courtesy of Musicmaker's Kits.

A thirty-one-string Gothic harp. Courtesy of Musicmaker's Kits.

NELSON & JACOBSON, INC.

3546 N. Clark St.
Chicago IL 60657

Nelson & Jacobson makes and sells the Electro bandsaw brazer, a tool that may seem totally beyond the needs of hobby woodworkers, but is nearly essential to anyone who depends on a bandsaw for major parts of their woodworking. This inexpensive (currently $89.75, F.O.B. factory) brazer allows quick making of new blades from coil bandsaw stock and rapid repair of broken blades. Operation is simple and quick and is easy enough to allow use of the bandsaw for internal sawing, which requires breaking and rebrazing the bandsaw blade.

NEWMAN

Box 46
New Braintree MA 01531   (508) 867-3318

Call or write for details on quartersawn lumber.

NIAGARA LUMBER & WOOD PRODUCTS, INC.

47 Elm St.   (800) 274-0397
East Aurora NY 14052   (716) 655-2142
                            FAX: (716) 655-2138

Northern Appalachian hardwoods are the primary product supplied by Niagara Lumber. Species include black cherry, tulip poplar, black walnut, basswood, birch, red oak, rock (hard) maple, mahogany (the only listed exotic), curly soft maple, white oak, white ash, butternut, and red elm. All lumber is kiln dried to a 6-8% moisture content, and surfacing is included at no extra cost. Don't forget when requesting surfacing that there is a thickness loss of at least 3/16" and more likely 1/4" in each dimension surfaced. One edge jointing is offered at $.12 a linear foot. Niagara also offers red oak and tulip poplar moldings and red oak tongue and groove flooring and paneling. Prices appear in line with other companies in the business. The brochure is free.

NORTH BAY FORGE

Box S
Waldron WA 98297

As with all hand-forged tools, North Bay's products tend to be pricey as compared to factory-made items. In many senses, it's a matter of choice when selecting tools, though a handmade tool has a greater beauty (and I don't think good machine-made tools are ugly at all, though cheaply made ones sure are) that is often worth the cost. With some makers, the beauty extends into the tool's handling. I can't comment on North Bay's tool handling, but the production is definitely by hand and in the old manner. North Bay Forge is located on Waldron Island, which has no phones (note the lack of phone number above) and lacks electricity! That doesn't mean no machines are used to produce North Bay Forge tools, but it does mean greater attention must be paid to each operation. The catalog, featuring scorps, draw-knives, and carver's knives, is free.

NORTHERN HYDRAULICS

P.O. Box 1219
Burnsville MN 55378   Order number: (800) 533-5545

Northern Hydraulics free 136-page catalog does have a lot of hydraulics equipment and parts, but there is a strong emphasis on hand and power tools as well. Lines carried include Milwaukee, Bosch, Skil, Makita, Channellock, their own NH, Hirsh, Vise-Grip, Homelite, Campbell-Hausfeld, Black & Decker, DeWalt, Ingersoll-Rand, and most others. If you wish to buy 250-pound capacity pneumatic 8" swiveling casters, I know of no other mail order source. There is a long ton of such stuff, including 1,500-pound industrial grade casters (I can't even imagine a woodworking need for such things, but probably someone, somewhere will). Prices are reasonable, and I have ordered from them often enough to state that their shipping times are also reasonable.

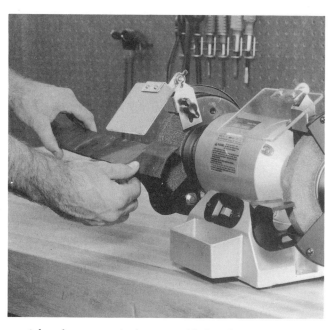

A bench mount grinder is notably handy and available by mail order. Courtesy of Skil Corp.

NORTHLAND WOODWORKING SUPPLY

65 Wurz Ave.   (315) 724-1299
Utica NY 13502   FAX: (315) 724-1298

Featuring Powermatic tools, Northland also offers free literature.

NOVA TOOL CO.

12500 Finnegan Rd.
P.O. Box 29341   Except NE:(800) 826-7606
Lincoln NE 68529   (402) 464-0511

Many woodworkers like to use a branding iron to let people know just who made a particularly fine piece. The Nova version is solid brass and costs $26.00 (plus $3.00 shipping and handling), or you may call or write for the free brochure.

OAK LUMBER CO.

1000 Cal Oak Rd.
Oroville CA 95965   (916) 534-1426

Write for their price list on hardwood flooring and wain-scoting.

OCS

Route 6   (800) 634-4047
Bethel CT 06801   (203) 792-8622

Give OCS a call for a free catalog of saw blades, listing a complete selection of scroll saw blades — skip tooth, double tooth, reverse tooth, spiral, metal cutting and pinned; bandsaw blades — flex back, hard back, furniture band and bi-metal; sandpaper in sheets, discs, and belts; plus books and accessories for scroll and band saw users.

ORNAMENTAL MOULDINGS LTD.

289 Marsland Dr.
P.O. Box 336
Waterloo ONT
Canada N2J 4A4   (519) 884-4080

Write or call for information on classic moldings.

OVERLAND, INC.

3023 E. 2nd St.
The Dalles OR 97058   (800) 345-6342

Write for free information on the Smithy mini-lathe.

OWINGS CRAFTS & GIFTS

Rt. 1, Box 255
Loranger LA 70446   (504) 878-4180

Send a large SASE for a list of wood cutouts.

P & M CONSUMER PRODUCTS

2423 W. March Lane
P.O. Box 7958   (800) 243-7010
Stockton CA 95267   (209) 957-6850

Call or write for information on cedar wainscoting.

WALTER PAC

Wood for Carvers and Furniture Makers
3505 32nd St. West
Bradenton FL 34205   (813) 756-5754

Walter Pac supplies blanks for carvers, ranging up from a 1"
x 1" x 2½" worry bird to duck decoys and on past to full-
sized carousel horses (and other animals; these may be any
size, not just ⅓ or full-sized). Prices range upward from $.75
for the smallest to $15.00 for a robin, nest, and three babies.
Decoy blanks run a dollar or two more, and larger kits are
custom priced. Of course, prices may also change over time,
so check with Walter even after getting his price list. Walter
Pac is also a source of cypress knees. The list is certainly
worth a self-addressed stamped envelope.

PACIFIC BURL & HARDWOOD

696 S.E. J St.
Grants Pass OR 97526   (503) 479-1854

Write or call for free samples and price list.

PACKARD WOODWORKS

P.O. Box 718
Tryon NC 28782

Packard is offering, for $1.00, a new catalog for woodturners,
listing tools, project supplies, books, videos, and more.

PENN STATE INDUSTRIES

2850 Comly Rd.   (800) 288-7297
Philadelphia PA 19154   (215) 676-7609

Penn State Industries presents a catalog of hobby woodworking machines in the low to moderate price range. Three
dust collector sizes are available, including a portable model
with a 760 cubic foot per minute capacity. Other machines,
including a 12" portable planer, a 6" x 48" belt sander with
9" disc, a three wheel bandsaw, a wood lathe, and a pile of
other tools and accessories that make the dust to be collected. The catalog is free and interesting.

PICKENS HARDWOODS

P.O. Drawer 1127
Clinton MS 39060-1127   (601) 924-4301

Call for information, or send $2.00 for the catalog and a
$2.00 refund coupon.

POOTATUCK CORP.

P.O. Box 24
Windsor VT 05089   (802) 674-5984

The maker of the Lion miter trimmer will send a free
brochure and price list on request. This guillotine-style
miter trimmer is exceptionally accurate and relatively low
cost. The tool uses razor sharp knives to do the trimming,
leaving a very smooth cut. Pootatuck sells by mail order, as
well as serving as manufacturer and distributor.

PRECISION MOVEMENTS

4251 Chestnut St.
Emmaus PA 18049   (215) 967-3156

Precision Movements specializes in clock movements and
clock-making supplies. Their 52-page catalog is free.

QUAKER STATE WOODWORKING SUPPLY

Airport Industries Bldg. #2
RD 9, Box 9386
Reading PA 19605

Quaker State Woodworking Supply offers plans, tools,
accessories, and a growing catalog/newsletter, currently in
the 16-page range. Drop a card to be added to the list for
their monthly publication.

RAINBOW WOODS

20 Andrews St.   (800) 423-2762
Newnan GA 30263   FAX: (404) 251-2761

Rainbow Woods offers hardwood turnings. In the free
Rainbow Woods catalog, you will find jewelry shapes,
jewelry findings ("hardware" to other woodworkers), hardwood dowels, dowel caps, wheels in many sizes, axle pegs,
smokestacks, all-purpose and tie rack pegs, barrels listed as
cargo, along with oil drums and milk cans, blocks from ½"
to 1½" square, peg people, round balls to 3" diameter,
candle cups, Shaker and mug pegs, furniture plugs and
buttons, dowel pins, fruits and vegetables, spools, pull
knobs, gallery rail spindles, larger birch spindles, salt and
pepper sets, and more. There may not be every turned wood
part available, but there are plenty for most purposes,
including wooden nickels, pill boxes, beads, buckets, and
stamp boxes. The catalog is fun, and the prices are reasonable.

RANDLE WOODS

Box 96
Randle WA 98377   (800) 845-8042

Quilted, curly, and other figured maples are among Randle's
featured woods, in boards, blocks, and flooring. Call for up-
to-date species lists and prices.

RBINDUSTRIES, INC.

1801 Vine St.	(800) 487-2623
P.O. Box 369	(816) 884-3534
Harrisonville MO 64701	FAX: (816) 884-2463

The RBI Hawk line of scroll saws is a good starting point for the tools made and sold by RBIndustries. These American-made scroll saws are among the best to be found, with throat capacities from 14" to 26", with the top three (of four) models produced as free-standing tools. RBI provides a complete line of scroll saw accessories, including a blade rack, diamond blades (for cutting glass and similar hard materials), and a drip tank system for cooling the diamond blade. RBI produces wood planers and a related tool they call the Panel Master, plus a drum sander 38" across, molding accessories for planers (the RBI planers can also be adapted as drum sanders and gang saws), dust collectors, a router table, and two versions of their Router Shop for producing dovetails, mortise and tenon, and other joints. Their catalog is free, and worth looking at. RBI sells by mail, as well as through other retail outlets.

RED HILL CORP.

P.O. Box 4234
Gettysburg PA 17325   (800) 822-4003

Red Hill offers a free 20-page finishing and refinishing products catalog, featuring major brands of abrasives in a wide range of available forms.

RENOVATOR'S SUPPLY

Millers Falls MA 01349

Customer service: (800) 659-3211
Order desk: (800) 659-2211
Corporate offices: (413) 659-2241

You're thinking that this is another nut entry, that a renovation supply place specializing in Victoriana is not of much help to woodworkers. Well, I would suggest you check a copy of their free catalog, especially if you need cabinet hardware that is a bit out of the ordinary. There are other items that are fascinating, but the cabinet hardware is most likely to be useful.

RJS CUSTOM WOODWORKING

P.O. Box 12354
Kansas City KS 66112

My listing for RJS started out noting they had toy carousel plans, but when I received their most recent catalog (printed on recycled paper, with a request that it be recycled after a new catalog arrives), I found that plans, including full-sized carousel plans and plans for dream car plaques (if your dream car is a Ferrari or a Rolls), are only a part of the line. Books range from Patrick Speilman's varied treatises on scroll saws, routers, and their uses, to his sign-making books, to R.J. De Cristoforo's array of power tool books (Cris's are among the best done to date), and on to wiring your own home. Products then range to a great many parts and pieces for projects, plus small tools. There are even stencils of many patterns, words, and letters (I believe most of these are Dover patterns).

This Ferris wheel was built from RJS Custom Woodworking plans.

ROOTS

Rural Route 3, Box 93A
Houston MN 55943

Send an SASE for a free brochure on manzanita roots.

ROYALWOOD LTD.

517 Woodville Rd.
Mansfield OH 44907   (419) 526-1630

If you need Shaker tape to complete a project, Royalwood has it. The $1.50 (refundable) catalog from this basket weaving and caning supplies mail order house presents extensive arrays of many items of great use in those fields. A Shaker Tape sample card is $2.00, as is a waxed linen color card; neither is refundable.

SAFETY SPEED CUT MANUFACTURING CO.

13460 N. Hwy. 65
Anoka MN 55304   (612) 755-1600

For years in the past, and very likely for years to come, I have wanted a plywood cutting panel saw such as those manufactured by SSC. There are features no hobby woodworker really needs, all of which tend to add to the cost, and these tools are expensive. But the lower cost models are dropping to within reason as time goes on (or my sense of the dollar's value is getting as warped as a politician's). Most of these are single-purpose machines that do nothing beyond ripping and crosscutting plywood. If you use much plywood, however, the savings in time, materials, energy, and the additions to safety, are quickly obvious. The least expensive model will take an 8' long panel at normal (48") width, and let you rip or crosscut with the panel in a vertical position. That means you are not feeding the heavy, unwieldy plywood panel into a table saw with all that does for inaccurate and unsafe cutting. The only other option is to use a circular saw to cut nearly to size, and then to finish cut on the table saw — this is what I usually do. It wastes material. Most of us use one or both of the above methods, but if you do a great deal of plywood work, give SSC a call or drop them a note and ask for their catalog. They sell directly and through dealers.

SANDY POND HARDWOODS

921 Lancaster Pike
Quarryville PA 17566   (717) 284-5030

As do many shipping lumber companies, Sandy Pond Hardwoods tends to specialize, in their case in tiger and bird's eye maple, curly ash, quartersawn oak, cherry, flame birch, and similar premium woods. In addition, Sandy Pond carries Northern red oak, white oak, hard maple and white hard maple, cherry, hickory, and ash in regular hardwoods. Figured woods, as noted, are usually premium price woods, but it pays to check the latest costs and availability. Sandy Pond also carries some exotic species, including mahogany, padauk, purple heart, wenge, bubinga, and a few others. Prices in their most recent list appear consistent with those of other companies. Call to request the most recent price list.

SANSHER CORPORATION

8005 N. Clinton St.
Fort Wayne IN 46825   (219) 484-2000

Sansher Corporation offers Dad's Drip Strip latex paint cleaner that also removes polyurethanes, lacquers, shellacs, varnishes, acrylics, paints, and epoxies. The remover is said to cut and dissolve like a liquid, while lifting and staying wet like a semi-gel, so that the stripping job may be stopped at any time, without waste or damage, for later resumption. It comes with its own chemical resistant sprayer, doesn't need a neutralizer, and is washed off with plain water, leaving no residue. I have not used this particular brand of remover, but if it does most of what is claimed, it will reduce work, odor, and mess considerably. Call or write the company for a brochure.

SECO INVESTMENTS COMPANY

315 Cloverleaf Dr. #C   (818) 333-1799
Baldwin Park CA 91706   FAX: (818) 333-1899

Seco manufactures and distributes primarily heavy-duty woodworking machinery, much of which is not going to interest hobby woodworkers. There are a number of exceptions, including a broad line of dust collectors from a 1 horse single phase unit up to a 10 horse three phase. Depending on the price, the 20" bandsaw might be of interest to some hobbyists, and they also have a good-looking (in the catalog) 10" table saw — 3 horsepower and single phase. Most of the rest of the machinery will remain as fantasy materials (many woodworkers would love a wide planer, but imagine the work installing the 5 horse, single phase 770 pound 20"). All the 24" models are three phase, which places them well out of the range of hobby shops. Seco also distributes a good-looking line of stock feeders. Literature is free, and worth asking for if you have any interest in the heavier woodworking machinery.

SEVEN CORNERS ACE HARDWARE, INC.

Tools On Sale Division
216 W. 7th St.   (800) 328-0457
St. Paul MN 55102   FAX: (612) 224-8263

Call the toll-free number to see what catalog is available. Tools On Sale presents a huge book, 416 pages long, listing discount prices on tools of virtually all brands. They carry everything from the Bessey clamping system and many Pony and Jorgenson clamps, Vise-Grip locking clamps, Bosch, Black & Decker, DeWalt, Makita, Milwaukee, Hitachi, Campbell-Hausfeld, Stanley-Bostitch, DeVilbiss, Ryobi, Skil, Porter-Cable, Delta, Freud, Fein, and many others in sanders, circular saws, table saws, radial arm saws, planers, router and shaper bits, Swiss army knives, all sorts of leather belts and pockets and tool holders, Plano tool boxes, Shop-Vac vacuums, and even extension cords.

SEYCO

1414 Cranford Dr.
Box 472749
Garland TX 75047-2749   (800) 462-3353

This scroll saw specialist has a $1.00 catalog.

SHAKER WORKSHOPS

Box 1028
Concord MA 01742
(617) 646-8985

Shaker furniture kits are shown in a 56-page catalog, along with twelve seat tape samples, for $1.00. The kits are also available completely finished.

STEVE H. WALL LUMBER CO.

Route 1, Box 287   (800) 633-4062
Mayodan NC 27027   (919) 427-0637
            FAX: (919) 427-7588

For $1.00 you get a lumber and machinery catalog that covers seventeen different woods, including ash, basswood, birch, butternut, cherry, hickory-pecan, real mahogany, hard maple, red and white oak, soft maple, walnut, and poplar. Softwoods include red cedar, cypress, and white and yellow pine. Listed prices for unsurfaced (rough) lumber seem in line with those I have seen lately. Freight charges make a major difference in cost, with woodworkers in the West getting hit hardest (currently, it costs $180 more to deliver 500 board feet of lumber to California than it does to most of the south and even up into Pennsylvania; for newcomers to woodworking, you can build a lot of pieces with 500 board feet of most any wood). That is a function of mileage that cannot change, so prices must be compared locally after shipping is figured. Steve H. Wall Lumber does offer some UPS specials in 20 board foot bundles of clear that may be of interest for those with small projects to complete. There are also special deals (log-run cherry surfaced two sides, to $^{13}/_{16}$", at $99.00 a hundred is the current deal, but these will vary). You will also find some Baltic birch $^{1}/_{8}$" plywood and veneer core hardwood plywoods at reasonable prices (I wish I had known their price for $^{3}/_{4}$" red oak veneer core before starting my current project!). Hardwood flooring is also available, as are Freud hand tools and an array of Mini Max stationary power tools, plus RBI's joint machine.

STEWART-MACDONALD

Box 900   (800) 848-2273
Athens OH 45701   FAX: (614) 593-7922

The 104-page free catalog from Stewart-MacDonald offers plans for a number of instruments: guitar (solid and acoustic bodies), mandolin, and banjo. Stewart-MacDonald also carries many odd tools and supplies (to me, with a lack of experience in this area of woodworking), including such products as fret tang nippers, three-corner fret files, bridge pin hole reamers, and similar items, which are at the least exotically named. Also offered are video courses in guitar repair, pearl inlay techniques, gluing secrets, guitar finishing, and more. To add to the line of information, Stewart-

MacDonald carries many tools other than those already mentioned, and goes on to carry a lot of familiar supplies (Hydrocote and Behlen finishes, HVLP spray finish outfits, dial calipers) amongst the bending irons, spool clamps, bridge clamps, bridge saddle routing jigs, and much more. They also carry the first actual vacuum tubes for amplifiers that I have seen in longer than I care to think about, as well as a couple of dulcimer kits that look interesting and not too difficult to build.

STONE MOUNTAIN POWER TOOL CORPORATION

6290 Jimmy Carter Blvd.   (404) 446-8390
Norcross GA 30071   FAX: (404) 416-6243

The tabloid size catalog — my most recent copy runs 32 large pages — presents an array of small and large power tools from all the major manufacturers (including Delta, Powermatic, Porter-Cable, Makita, Ryobi, Bosch, Panasonic, AccuSpray, Stanley-Bostitch, Hitachi, Williams & Hussey, etc.), plus many accessories, bits, and blades. There is a note in the catalog to call if you don't see what you want. Stone Mountain Power Tools also has a retail store (Norcross is just north of Atlanta) and presents a seminar schedule for each of the four seasons, with eight or ten subjects, including projects, processes, and tool use (mostly router use in the current catalog).

DeWalt's new DW705 12" miter saw cuts crown molding to 5¼" wide and regular molding to 7⅞" wide at 45 degrees. It is available from many mail order outlets. Courtesy of Black & Decker.

SUN DESIGNS

173 E. Wisconsin Ave.
Oconomowoc WI 53066 (414) 567-4255

Sun Designs is a small company producing design books and construction plans for yard and other projects. Strom Toys is considered a classic of toy design and making and is one of the products from Sun. Janet Strombeck kindly sent along blueprints for the Victoria, a truly lovely sleigh, and a copy of *Timeless Toys In Wood* for me to examine. If I still lived in an area with decent amounts of winter weather — snow, for example — I would quickly build the Victoria, and go further and produce the Bunker Hill sled. Even without a local winter wonderland, I find plenty of toy plans. The engine and coal car in Timeless Toys are an ex-

ample; large enough to provide riding models for small children, with enough accessories and other cars to keep a woodworking parent or grandparent busy for a long time. The designs shown in *Gazebos and Other Garden Structures* will keep many a woodworker or carpenter employed for an even longer period. *Gazebos* is an idea book, with plans for the most part available as extra attractions, at varying prices (birdhouse or feeder plans, for example, are about $5.95 each; buy more, get a discount per plan; gazebo plans are $24.95 each). You'll see drawings with some of the plans, many of which are ornate and correspondingly difficult to build. Others are less ornate and less difficult to erect. The four-color brochure is $.50. Sun Designs also mail orders accessory packages for their toy designs.

Sun Designs' rocking horse plans allow production of a superb toy.

Sun Designs' doll carriage may be the ultimate project to present to a little girl.

Sun Designs' projects also include plans for a fancy dog house.

TALARICO HARDWOODS

RD 3, Box 3268
Mohnton PA 19540   (800) 373-6097

Wide quartersawn oak boards and figured lumber are featured at Talarico Hardwoods. Call for species and price quotes.

TASHIRO'S

1024 S. Bailey St.
Seattle WA 98108   (206) 762-8242

Tashiro's has been importing Japanese tools for over a century and offers a solid array of saw blades and handles, for almost all wood-cutting purposes. The catalog is free, and contains instruction on selecting the right blade for the job, and using the proper handle for the blades needed.

TATRO, INC.

7011 Marcelle   (800) 748-5827
Paramount CA 90723   FAX: (310) 630-6668

Tatro's free catalog shows many, many wood turnings and shapes, from the old standard Shaker pegs, in birch and oak, to checkers, snowmen, eggs, egg cups, wood scoops, napkin rings, beads (in colors, as well as plain wood), wheels, cargo pieces (barrels, milk cans, milk bottles, drums), stamp boxes, needle boxes, vanity boxes, necklace kits, spindles, finials, fruits, and much else.

TIMBERS COUNTRY STORE

P.O. Box 897
Wheatley ONT   (819) 825-7480
Canada N0P 2P0   FAX: (819) 825-3780

I first heard of Timbers Country Store as a source for doll house parts and plans, and a single page certainly proves that to be the case, with cedar shakes, siding, and a line of windows and doors that looks very interesting. They have a special order setup and catalog that provide much more. Added to the doll house plans and parts there are game plans and parts and many, many kinds of plans for furniture, toys, and other items. Timbers also sells hardware, small tools, clock kits, accessories for just about anything, including lamp kits, books, wood parts, musical movements, and whirligig parts. The catalog is free. It's difficult to judge Canadian prices from the U.S. because I don't keep track of exchange rates, but I imagine your bank, or Timbers Country Store, can give any U.S. customers an angle on the rates.

TOOL CHEST

45 Emerson Plaza   (201) 261-8665
East Emerson NJ 07630   FAX: (201) 261-3865

The $2.00 Tool Chest catalog offers thousands of books, most new but some used. Catalog price is refundable. The company also sells new and used hand and power tools of all types, including antique, along with almost all accessories, from eye shields to saw blades to drill bits and waxes and more. Most accessories are new. Generators, sprayers, and large machinery are also sold. Rentals, warranty, and after warranty repairs are offered.

THE TOOL COMPANY

812 Kurzeil Rd.
Raymore MO 64083   (816) 537-6308

The Tool Company features the Wheelwright, a cutter for wooden wheels that works on drill presses to produce toy wheels from wood scraps. Three different size cutters are available (one size supplied with the basic tool). The $1.00 catalog offers other items as well.

Veritas tools are available from most mail order sources.

TOOL CRIB OF THE NORTH

Box 1716   (800) 358-3096
Grand Forks ND 58206   FAX: (701) 746-2857

The $3.00 200+-page Tool Crib catalog shows a wide, wide range of tools, from the AccuMiter to Vega fence systems, with listings in between for Black & Decker, Freud, Milwaukee, Porter-Cable, Makita, Bosch, Delta, General, S-K, Custom Leathercraft, Vise-Grip, HTC, Porta-Nails, Ridgid, Jet, Shop-Vac, Elu, DeWalt, Ryobi, Skil, Senco, and many more, including books, levels, jigs, HVLP sprayers, glues, etc.

TOYS AND JOYS

P.O. Box 682
Lyndon WA 98264

The $1.00 Toys and Joys catalog expands on a list of patterns, wheels, pegs, dowels, and kits with the aim being primarily wooden vehicles that are extremely nicely detailed.

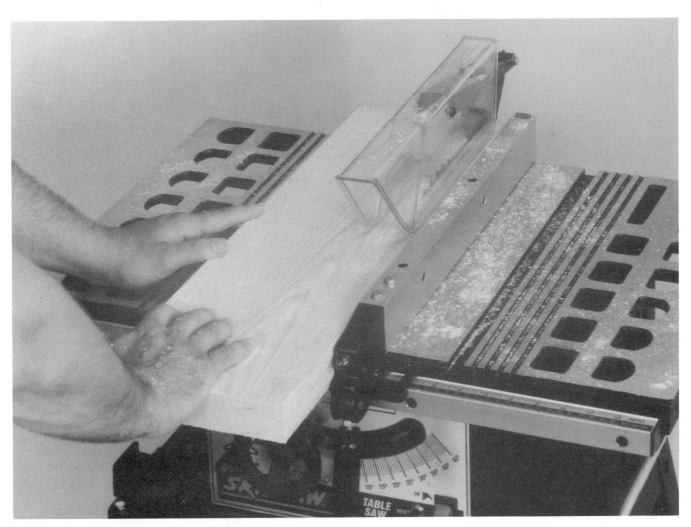

Skil's 10" benchtop table saw is another mail order item. The light weight and relatively small size of benchtop tools make most of them easy to ship by United Parcel Service.

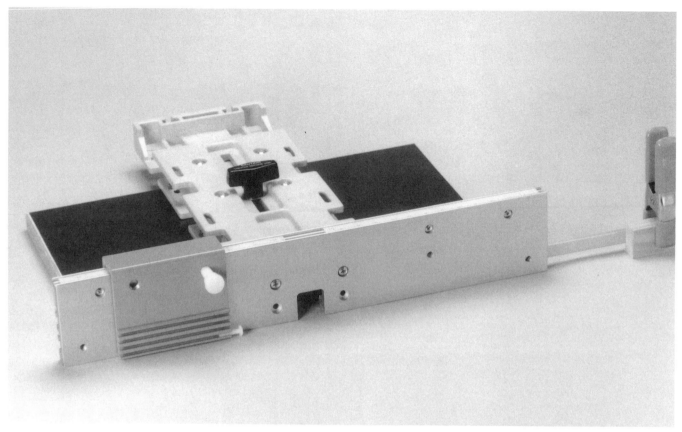

The original Incra Jig is available from mail order sources.

TREND-LINES

375 Beacham St.   Catalog request number:
Chelsea MA 02150   (800) 366-6966

Trend-Lines is a discount mail order house and the distributor of the Reliant line of power tools. Their catalog ranges from Dremel to Delta, through Ryobi, Panasonic, Black & Decker, Bostitch, Campbell-Hausfeld, Fuji (HVLP), Freud, Nikon, Record, Marples, Grant, Porter-Cable, Makita, ITW-Paslode, Senco, DML, PNI, Oldham, Performax, and a slew of others. Their free catalog presents more than 3,000 brand-name products, including power tools and accessories, hand tools, screws, hardware, wood parts, plans, books, and more. The current issue, as always, emphasizes tools, including roller work stations, a new, industrial-style 10" table saw, much of the new DeWalt line of portable power tools, and goes on to raised panels for drawer fronts and doors, dowels, wood threading kits, and glues, among a wide variety of items. It also includes Porter-Cable's new Laser Loc 10" miter saw (an item I've recently tried: that fast-moving either-side-of-the-blade laser line *really* puts you on your mark). Stan Black always has some interesting tools, often some new tools, and produces a catalog that packs a lot

of interest for just about all woodworkers. Complete satisfaction guarantee.

TROPICAL EXOTIC HARDWOODS

Box 1806   (619) 434-3030
Carlsbad CA 92018   FAX: (619) 434-5423

For this importer of hardwoods, a self-addressed stamped envelope (#10) brings a list of available woods. Available are (not all tropical, of course) fiddleback ash, bocote, bloodwood, canary wood, cocobolo, African ebony, goncalo alves, granodillo Cristobal, jatoba, Mexican kingwood, lignum vitae, Cuban mahogany, mansonia, bird's eye maple, partridgewood, pink ivory, primavera, purple heart, Brazilian rosewood, Ceylon satinwood, snakewood, teak, Brazilian tulipwood, and ziricote. Some is sold by the pound. Wood is available in different sizes, but usually in 4/4, 6/4, 8/4, cants (half logs), crotches, and other normal forms. Lumber is 3" or wider and 3' or longer, air dried, and unsurfaced unless otherwise specified. For lumber 8" and wider, Tropical Exotic Hardwoods charges a 15% premium. Prices are F.O.B. Carlsbad, CA. Call and check for the latest prices, methods of avoiding C.O.D. shipment, and so on.

Trend-Lines markets its Reliant bandsaw by mail (but it must be delivered by truck: this is not *a bench-top tool).*

TURNCRAFT

P.O. Box 100
Mound MN 55364-0100   (800) 544-1711

This is a new addition to the lineup of mail order companies, specializing in different and unusual, as well as traditional, clock parts and clock plans. The catalog displays a variety of quartz movements, with and without pendulums and chimes, and an even wider variety of clock faces in sizes from 3¾" up to 12⅜". Drop a line and request the catalog if you are at all interested in making reasonably simple clocks.

UNICORN STUDIOS

P.O. Box 370
Seymour TN 37865

The full-line Unicorn catalog, for $1.00, features musical movements in one of the largest tune selections anywhere,

many of which are hard to find, even a few that are unique to Unicorn.

UNICORN UNIVERSAL WOODS LTD.

4190 Steeles Ave. W.
Woodbridge ONT   (416) 851-2308
Canada L4L 3S8   FAX: (416) 851-8039

This Canadian outfit doesn't deal in the hard facts of woods, thus their brochure is a listing of woods available and the prices (for U.S. dollars, prices are currently 15% less). There are also some solid facts on American forest resources, with emphasis on the Canadian and South American forests. Hardwood plank flooring in ash, birch, cherry, hickory, maple, mahogany, oak, sassafras, and walnut, with price per board foot dropping rapidly as board footage escalates. Paneling and siding in butternut, cedar, pine, and redwood are all available, as are many kinds of moldings in cherry, walnut, red gum, mahogany, maple, ash, white and red oak, clear pine, and poplar. Rough lumber covers the above named species and many, many others, including greenheart, blackwood, boxwood, jelutong, hornbeam, holly, cordia, spruce, thuya, sycamore, yew, and many others. Unicorn Universal also carries plywoods, many types of veneer, burls, crotches, and inlays, plus edge tape and butcher block and countertop glue-ups. Check the free brochure.

UNIVERSAL CLAMP COMPANY

15200 Stagg St.
Van Nuys CA 91405   (818) 780-1015

The Universal face frame clamp series offers woodworkers light weight and good durability in clamps with great versatility. The adjustable bar clamp series comes in five sizes (24", 36", 48", 60", and 72"), and they work right up to the specified length, which is not always the case with clamps. The flat back of the UC-900 clamps allows them to be placed on floor or bench, and the work set right on them. Other UC clamps offer wedge grips for security and allow for easy positioning on a wide variety of stock sizes. One item I like is the UC-Featherboard. This featherboard slips right into the ¾" (standard size, but not universal, so check) wide miter slot of a table saw and serves as a featherboard when clamped down. I have a couple and use them frequently. The company has been serving woodworkers since 1969. Write or call for a copy of the Universal Clamp brochure, though they sell through mail order houses, hardware stores, and the like.

VAN DYKE'S RESTORERS

Woonsocket SD 57385

(800) 843-3320
(605) 796-4425
(605) 796-4085

This company, selling mostly upholsterer's, refinisher's, and restorer's supplies, offers their wholesale catalog for $1.00. I must admit to interest, though I thought there would not be much. The first point that piqued that interest was the cutline on the letter that came with it: "The World's Largest Supplier & Manufacturer of Glass Eyes." That is simply intriguing, so I had to dive right into the catalog to see what else went on. And plenty does. For any woodworker doing cabinetry, this catalog is a help. Wooden knobs. Hardware in general, including a huge line of solid, cast brass, gives you a start, and reproduction hardware from many areas continues on. There are wheels, toy maker's supplies and doll house shingles, pegs and turning squares in walnut and other woods, carving wood, tea cart wheels, oak doorstops, lumber, veneer, and deer photographs (?), wooden duck carving kits, oil and electric lamp kits, marble knobs, embossed seats, artificial fur, and vinyl and glass eyes. Oh yes, there are glass eyes! There are faceted glass jewel eyes and carousel horse eyes and doll eyes, pinpoint pupil eyes (available in all colors, which include hazel, straw, yellow, red, black, blue,

and green) and owl eyes, and novelty carnival eyes and true profile veined eyes, and ... shoot. Send for the catalog. It's a ball and has a lot of useful stuff, including much of the above, as well as caning materials, books, and so on.

VERITAS TOOLS

12 E. River St.
Ogdensburg NY 13669

(613) 596-1922
Office: (613) 596-0350
FAX: (613) 596-3073

The variety of interesting and useful tools that comes from Veritas is close to astounding. At the outset, there is a tendency to think of less expensive formed plastic tools, such as the center marker, the tool setting gauge, and the poly gauge. That notion quickly slides away as you note, on moving away from the pair of simple corner rounding tools to the edge trimming block plane, the Veritas shelf drilling jig, at over $100.00, or the Tucker vise, at $495.00. The Tucker vise may need some justification, other than its 13" wide jaws, 4" throat, 5½" wide side jaws with 4½" throat, 2¾" wide carver's chop jaws with 6" throat depth, double ⅞" guide rods, and 12" opening for all jaws, so consider it allows full rotation and tilt, has integral dogs (four 6" round

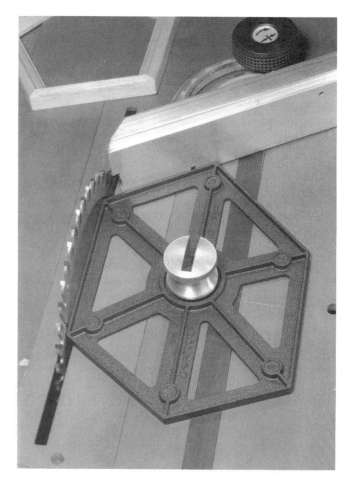

Veritas angle gauge speeds setting popular angles.

Van Dyke's recent catalog cover.

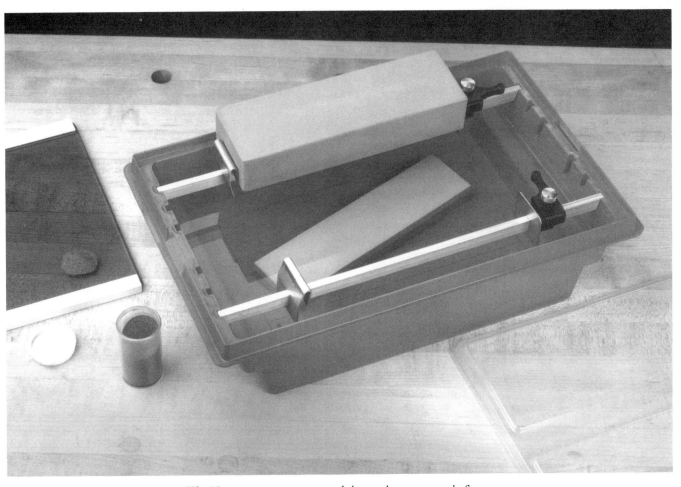

The Veritas water stone trough keeps the stones ready for use.

The Veritas angle gauge also works erect.

dogs: two in each jaw), pivoting front jaw, automatic opening, quick-release, lined jaws (cork), elevated guide rods, and much more. It is, in fact, the epitome of current woodworkers' vises. Whether or not it's worth 500 bucks depends on you (*Popular Mechanics* presented the Tucker

Vise with its Design and Engineering award in January 1992).

WARREN TOOL COMPANY

2209-1 Rt. 9G
Rhinebeck NY 12572   (914) 876-7817

Fred Clark offers a multiplicity of carving tools, with interchangeable blades for the many handles, and a variety of kits. Warren Tool also carries sharpening tools for most carving implements, books, sharpening accessories, and related tools. Fred's line of carving knives seems especially wide, and he offers a basic woodcarving kit with a book, a handle, a small blade, and a basswood cutout for less than $16.00. The catalog is $1.00.

WEST FALLS WOODCARVING

7458 Ellicott Rd.
West Falls NY 14170   (716) 662-3648

Send an SASE for a brochure on carving blanks and rough-outs.

WEST FRIENDSHIP HARDWOODS

P.O. Box 103
West Friendship MD 21794

Send for a free price list of micro-thin hardwoods.

WHOLESALE GLASS BROKERS

19785 W. Twelve Mile Rd.
Suite 357
Southfield MI 48076   (800) 288-6854

For dining and coffee table tops, shelves, partitions, cabinet doors, beveled panels, or any rectangular, square, circular, or hole-drilled glass, in clear, bronze, gray, from ¼" to 1" thick, including tempered glass, call or write to check out the free catalog and price guide.

Vaughan & Bushnell's hollow core fiberglass handle on the FS16 curved claw hammer absorbs shock well.

WILKE MACHINERY COMPANY

3230 Susquehanna Trail   (717) 764-5000
York PA 17402   FAX: (717) 764-3778

Bridgewood woodworking machinery is featured in the Wilke catalog and starts with an emphasis on the big guns, their 24" x 9" planer being the lead-off item. At a net weight of 1,910 pounds, this might go through the floor in more than a few shops I know. A few pages on, we run into small shop tools with a 20" economy planer (still 771 pounds), then to the 15" planer, and on to the 12" portable model (64 pounds net). Throughout, there is a choice of huge, medium, and small shop items (except for those items that aren't at all suitable to small shops, such as 4-side moulders, and 3-side planer-moulders, tenoners and so on). The current sale price on the Bridgewood 20½" floor drill press is a stunner. You might check for later examples of such sales. The catalog is $1.00 (free in the showroom) and well worth checking out.

WILLARD BROTHERS WOODCUTTERS

300 Basin Rd.
Trenton NJ 08619   (609) 890-1990

Willard Brothers sawmill offers domestic and exotic hardwoods, cabinet plywoods, veneers, finishes, Freud tools, mulch, and Christmas trees. My price list came with a notice of an annual auction and sale, with 25,000+ board feet of quality hardwoods, in more than 200 stacks of kiln- and air-dried walnut, maple, cherry, white and red oak, poplar, ash, pine, birch, and others. The price list offers domestic species that include the above, butternut, aromatic red cedar, both bird's-eye and curly maple, and sassafras. Prices appear in line with others carrying domestic woods lines. Exotics include Australian lacewood, bocote, Brazilian kingwood and tulipwood, bubinga, chechen, cocobolo, ebony, mahogany, morado, padauk, purple heart, rosewood, teak, shedua, wenge, zebrawood, and others. Prices for domestic woods are difficult to judge, but these appear reasonable. The sawmill charges a premium of $.25 a board foot on widths 10" and greater (8" and greater with black walnut). Flipping the page brings a supplemental list that includes sycamore, cypress, anegre, spalted maple, nogal, clear pine, redwood, and types of cherry, oak, birch, and poplar molding, as well as mahogany, oak, cherry, and soft maple wainscoting. Worth a look.

WILLIAMS & HUSSEY MACHINE CO., INC.

Riverview Mill   (800) 258-1380
P.O. Box 1149   (603) 654-6828
Wilton NH 03086   FAX: (603) 654-5446

The W&H molder-planer unit offers quick blade changes, and a capacity of almost double blade width because one side is open, allowing double pass cutting. The unit also takes molding cutting blades, to double utility. The W&H lathe is relatively low cost and high precision. Write or call for free information kit.

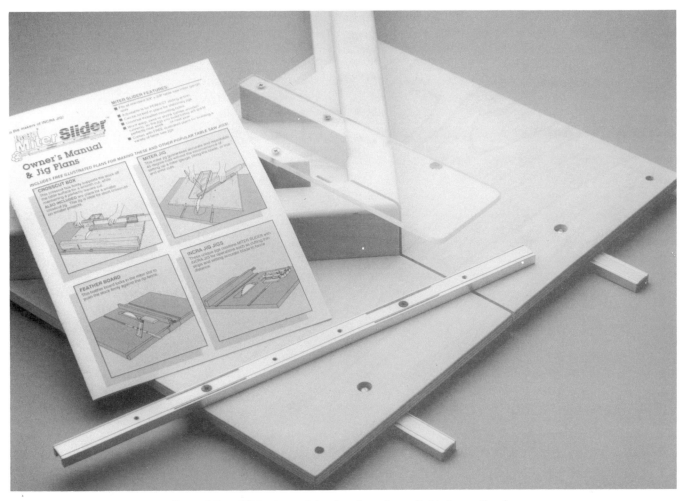

Incra Miter Slider is a mighty handy tool, available by mail order.

This fast-cutting 24 tooth blade is from Irwin.

WILLIAMS TOOL & HARDWARE SUPPLY

2017 White Settlement Rd.
Fort Worth TX 76107   (800) 338-6668

Mail order general woodworking tools and supplies, including Amana router bits, Incra system jigs and rigs, Porter-Cable, Dremel, Ryobi, Makita, Bosch, Delta, and Hitachi power tools, ready-to-assemble drawers, roller stands, Freud and Delta blades, plans, books, sanding drums, abrasive accessories, wood parts, and Olson scroll saw blades. Catalog is free.

JOHN WILSON

500 E. Broadway Hwy.
Charlotte MI 48813   (517) 543-5325

John is the modern day torch bearer for Shaker oval boxes, and offers everything from instruction sheets to the kits to make the boxes, right up to and including the correct kind of toothpicks to use as pegging. A typical Shaker oval box kit will include materials for the lid, box bands (bent to shape), and wood for the bottom, plus an instruction sheet. You need only provide wood glue, a saw that will cut an oval, 120 and 220 grit sandpaper, and clear finish. He has his own video and a line of tools, accessories, and patterns that makes the overall job a great deal simpler. John also has a pattern packet that presents more than two dozen oval boxes and carriers, and he offers workshops at specific intervals during the year, at varied places, so you don't always have to be in Michigan to learn to make oval boxes. Give him a call, or drop a note, to check prices of current literature and workshops.

which is what Pete teaches. Paul White is the blacksmith and makes tools ranging from spoonbit adzes to deep curve travishers. (He also makes slight curve travishers, which are meant for final finishing of chair seats, while the deep curve tool does the heavy work.) Paul will also replicate almost any hand tool used in the 18th and 19th centuries. His brochure is free and interesting, and prices do not seem out of line for quality handmade tools. As of March 1993, Paul will also be shipping rived wood for Windsor chair seats.

Adzing a Windsor chair seat. Courtesy of Windsor Forge.

Irwin spade bits are great for fast boring and are mail order items.

WINDSOR FORGE

1403 Harlem Blvd.
Rockford IL 61103   (815) 964-9590

Located across the street from Pete Cullum's Dovetail Joint school of Windsor chairmaking, the Windsor Forge offers complementary items — the tools with which to make such chairs and many of the parts already cut. This is a 19th century production blacksmith shop producing tools to make 19th century chairs using 19th century techniques,

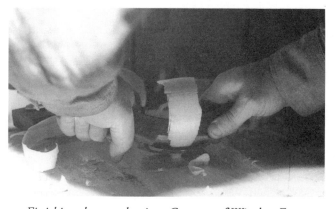

Finishing the seat shaping. Courtesy of Windsor Forge.

Windsor Forge tools and hand-scooped Windsor chair seat.

WINTER WOODS

Route 1, Box 765G
Munising MI 49862   (906) 387-4082

Winter Woods specializes in figured woods, such as tiger (soft maple) and bird's eye (hard) maple, burls, and spalted lumber. In addition to the maples, they carry curly aspen, curly cherry, and basswood carving blocks. Prices vary depending on figure, wood species, etc., but those listed appear in line with prices charged elsewhere. Call or write for their free brochure.

WOLFE MACHINERY CO.

6107 Merle Hay Rd.   (800) 345-6659
P.O. Box 497   (515) 270-2766
Johnston IA 50131   FAX: (515) 270-0628

Wolfe Machinery is an authorized Lancaster service center for DeWalt radial arm saws and services and sells much other woodworking machinery, including SSC (Safety Speed Cut) panel saws and panel routers. Wolfe will service equipment, sell and set up new equipment, do on-site breakdown repairs, in-shop reconditioning, remachine radial arms, rewind motors, and fabricate obsolete parts. The list of tool brands sold is close to total, from Alden gang rip saws (not too handy for the hobby woodworker) to Wilson radial arm saws, running through Delta, Powermatic, Biesemeyer fences, Systematic saw blades, and Wisconsin Knife Works saw blades. Free brochure.

WOOD CARVERS SUPPLY, INC.

P.O. Box 7500-V
Engelwood FL 34295   (813) 698-0123

This national mail order outfit has served woodcarvers since 1955. Products in the catalog include over 2,000 woodcarving supplies, such as hand and power carving tools, kits, books, knives, wood. The 76-page catalog is rush shipped for $1.00. Wood carvers may also want to inquire about the Global Carving Challenge. This annual event offers over $15,000 cash and prizes.

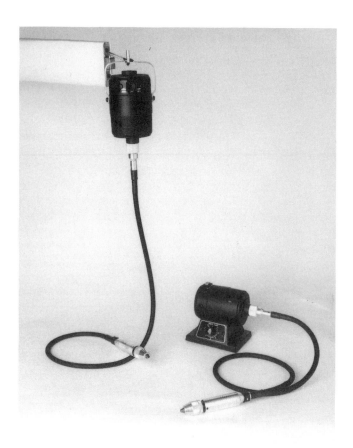

Wood Carver's Supply power carving tool.

WOODHAVEN

5323 W. Kimberly   (800) 344-6657
Davenport IA 52806   (319) 391-2386

Woodhaven is a fairly old (past a decade) mail order house for router bits, tables, and general router supplies. Their router base plate is offered in four basic styles, and may be modified to fit jig saws in one style. Inlay templates for construction of your own router table tops are also offered, as are fences, angle brackets, and a slew of interesting items for the router-using woodworker. The Woodhaven miter and box joint jig is a neat item, from appearances and reports. For dowel-making jigs, vacuum clamp kits, Keller dovetailing jigs, Beall wood threaders, and an array of other items, this catalog offers much of interest to the woodworker. One such item is the Know-Bit. This is not much more than a pointed metal dowel, with the point set to the top when inserted in a router. It then serves as an exact centering device for router, drill press, and lathe. It is machined perfectly straight and round, so also makes a good run-out (wobble) check when used with a dial indicator.

Chuck it into your drill press, router, or lathe, and quickly and simply measure the run-out. The catalog is $3.00 by first class mail or free by bulk mail.

WOOD-MIZER PRODUCTS, INC.

8180 W. 10th St.   (800) 553-0182
Indianapolis IN 46214   (317) 271-1542

Wood-Mizer is your company if you are truly sick of paying high prices for good lumber. The company makes portable sawmills of the bandsaw type (generally a bit lower in cost — though far from inexpensive for the good ones, which this is — than circular sawmill setups, as well as being more portable). There are six versions, and the catalog then goes on to describe Solar Dry kilns to finish up the work. Actually, the smallest Solar Dry kiln is not wildly expensive (again, though, it depends on your state of interest, and wallet: delivered, it will probably run about $2,250, with a current price of $2,090), and will dry 750 board feet at a time. The third product line is the Dupli-Carver used to produce three-dimensional wood carving duplicates. The catalog is free and fascinating.

WOOD-N-CRAFTS

Box 140
Lakeview MI 48850

Send for a free catalog of wood products—wheels, pegs, and similar items.

WOODENBOAT STORE

P.O. Box 78   (800) 225-5205
Brooklin ME 04616   FAX: (207) 359-8920

The WoodenBoat name tells the story. This store caters to wooden boat enthusiasts, those who build, buy, sail, or row such devices, and the catering is extensive. Books on the subject of wooden boats, both appreciation and construction, and more than a few on use, abound. Plans for model boats and even kits for model boats, a couple of which are over three feet long, are offered. There are numerous plans for a wide variety of wooden craft, ranging from a 7'7" pram to a 41'3" schooner, with the list including daysailers, power launches, rowing shells, kayaks, and canoes. There are also boat kits, for Nutshell prams in two sizes (9'6" and 7'7"), and the usual batch of logo T-shirts and sweatshirts. The handiest logo item is the WoodenBoat shop apron. The most fascinating item in the entire catalog, to me, is the Friendship sloop sailing model. This model finishes up at 7'7" along the deck and sails much like a real boat. The original is 29' long. The store is an offshoot of *WoodenBoat* magazine and offers similar quality and interests. If you love boats, this catalog is for you. If you love boats and woodworking, jump on it.

slides from Blum, lazy Susan setups for cabinetry of many kinds, organizer rails for compact discs, videotapes, and audio cassettes. There are casters, cable hole covers, glass door hinges, halogen lights, oak wood moldings, gallery rails and spindles, Shaker pegs, mug pegs, desk top fasteners, and more. It is essential that you check to see what is available, for we don't have the space to even name it all.

WOODWORKERS' STORE

21801 Industrial Blvd.   (612) 428-2199
Rogers MN 55374-9514   FAX: (612) 428-8668

Another major mail order source for many items, The Woodworkers' Store carries a wide line of small power tools, hand tools, woods, finishes, plans, jigs, kits, and a very wide line of hardware, including many porcelain parts, oak and birch carvings, and even briefcase handles in two quality levels (the cheaper is covered in vinyl, the more costly in leather). Currently unique is their line of workshop knobs in black plastic or aluminum, in five styles and many more sizes. The knobs make building your own shop jigs a great deal easier, as do some other new kits in the most recent catalog. You will also find a large line of jewelry box, chest and drawer, and general cabinet locks, and plenty of knock-

Building a canoe of wood. Courtesy of WoodenBoat School.

WOODPECKERS

8318 Manorford Dr.   (800) 752-0725
P.O. Box 29510   (216) 888-6332
Parma OH 44129   FAX: (216) 888-9463

This company offers a wide line of products, including the US/Procut line of router bits, the full line of Incra products, and many others. I can't do much more of a review, because I caught them with their catalogs down — for revision. The catalog is free, so give them a call and request one.

WOODWORKER'S HARDWARE

P.O. Box 784
St. Cloud MN 56302   (800) 383-0130

This free catalog of cabinet and furniture hardware is huge, running upwards of 155 pages. There appears to be something for everyone here, with everything from Hafele oak drawer pulls to wrought iron reproduction Colonial hardware, wire bail pulls, Amerock epoxy-coated drawer slides, wall standards and brackets, pivot door slides, pocket door

Tagua nuts now replace ivory for inlay and carving work. Courtesy of The Woodworkers' Store.

down fasteners. The Woodworkers' Store is another company that sends smaller update catalogs with some frequency, so your $3.00 buys a great deal of information. The Woodworkers' Store operates eleven retail outlets in Boston, Chicago, Cleveland, Columbus, Denver, Detroit, Milwaukee, Minneapolis, San Diego, Seattle, and Buffalo. The retail stores *do not* accept mail order, but may speed access to some items if you happen to be nearby.

WOODWORKER'S SUPPLY

5604 Alameda Place N.E.	(800) 645-9292
Albuquerque NM 87113	(505) 821-0578

Not only does Woodworker's Supply offer a wide variety of tools and project supplies, it offers three different stores, with one in Casper, Wyoming (307) 237-5528, and another in Graham, North Carolina (919) 578-0500. They offer Woodtek stationary tools in addition to the standard lines from Delta and other makers. The widest catalog line offered is the Woodtek, with machines going right up to professional woodbanding machines, overarm routers, and a moderately priced joint-making machine called Matchmaker. One page of plans contains a number of interesting Southwestern furniture plans, including a Solana bed, Taoseno daybed, bookshelf, nightstand, wardrobe, and table plans.

WOODWORKERS SOURCE

5402 S. 40th St.	(800) 423-2450
Phoenix AZ 85040	(602) 437-4415

This lumber producer offers hardwoods, plywoods, and exotics, such as Brazilian cherry and purple heart. Call or write for free brochure.

WOODWORKS

P.O. Box 14507	(800) 722-0311
Ft. Worth TX 76117	(817) 281-4447

If you need small hardware or wood parts, the $1.00 catalog contains a good listing of each, including spoked wheels, buttons, dowels, spindles, and many more.

SECTION IV

EDUCATION, PLANS, PUBLICATIONS, VIDEOS, ASSOCIATIONS AND GUILDS

Education — Courses and Classes for Woodworkers

AMERICAN ASSOCIATION OF WOODTURNERS

667 Harriet Ave.
Shoreview MN 55126   (612) 484-9094

The AAW offers symposia on wood turning and is an international non-profit organization aimed at advancing woodturning. In essence, the Association provides information, education, and organization to those interested in lathe work, through a quarterly journal, *American Woodturner*, the membership directory, and other benefits, including the symposia. General membership is $25.00 annually. You may also contact them for dates and places of events.

BEREA COLLEGE CRAFTS

CP0 2347
Berea KY 40404

You may write Berea College for more information on their crafts program, or send $2.00 for their color crafts catalog. Berea has long been recognized as one of the top crafts schools, providing a top liberal arts education as well (as my oldest stepdaughter can attest, with her honors degree in Latin). The school offers a special chance for students to experience what it is to work for what one gets: there are no charges for tuition and fees, with expenses, including at least part of room and board, met by student earnings. Every student works at least ten to fifteen hours weekly while carrying a full academic courseload. The crafts program began in 1893, with the Fireside Weaving course, and now includes Weaving and Needlecraft, Ceramics, Broomcraft, and Wrought Iron. The Woodcraft program is renowned throughout the industry. In all craft courses, students work side by side with master craftsmen (and women, I assume).

COLLEGE OF THE REDWOODS

440 Alger St.
Fort Bragg CA 95437   (707) 964-7056

Fine Cabinetmaking courses directed by James Krenov and Michael Burns are featured. Call or write for information.

DOVETAIL JOINT

1332 Harlem Rd.
Rockford IL 61103   (815) 965-6677

Write for information on five-day classes in Windsor chair making and Shaker furniture workshops taught by Peter Cullum. Pete didn't provide tuition figures but will on your copy of the brochure: tuition includes five nights lodging and meals served at the Cullum home. Pete teaches hand- and foot-operated tool methods, and students get to use his shop full of such tools. Class size is small for maximum one-on-one instruction, so there is no need for students to be expert woodworkers already.

HYMILLER SCHOOL OF FINE FINISHING & HAND JOINERY

Route 2, Box 243A
Sparta TN 38583   (615) 738-5706

John Hymiller offers an impressive list of references for the school he teaches. From his other advertising, he appears to specialize in restoration of truly messed up antiques but also builds and finishes fine furniture when not teaching. The course offered — fine finishing, repair, and hand joinery — is two weeks long, with the first week devoted to everything from marketing through fine finishing in lacquer. The student finishes four miniature table tops as examples of his or her work. Week two moves from sharpening to cabinet scrapers to hand cut dovetails, mortises and tenons, and making proper glue joints. Courses are limited to three students for direct, hands-on supervision. Currently, the price is $950.00 a week, including materials.

NORTHWEST SCHOOL OF WOODEN BOATBUILDING

251 Otto St.   (206) 385-4948
Port Townsend WA 98368   (206) 385-5089

The Northwest School of Wooden Boatbuilding offers a variety of one-week seminars and weekend workshops, plus a six-month core program. Seminars are five to six days long, at $300 each (plus $50 registration and varied text and materials costs). Workshops are listed at $35.00 each, and cover such subjects as steam bending, oar making, planking, interior joinery (you will probably never learn more about joinery than when working on a boat, with its odd angles and curves and need for extreme conservation of space), wood turning, spar making, tools, and more. If you are going to be or can be in the area for one or more of these workshops or seminars (small boat construction and wooden boat repair are probably of most interest to woodworkers), drop a line and ask for their catalog materials.

OREGON SCHOOL OF ARTS & CRAFTS

8245 SW Barnes Rd.
Portland OR 97225   (503) 297-5544

Woodworking is but a single facet of the Oregon School of Arts & Crafts program, but the school offers both an open program and a certificate program in woodworking. The Certificate program is one developed by artists, for artists, and takes three years, including a business practices curriculum along with the arts curriculum. Additional subjects of value to the artist include grant writing and presenting and marketing work. There currently are ten woodworking courses listed, starting with first year fundamentals and ending with individualized wood study. Write or call for information.

PETERS VALLEY CRAFT CENTER

19 Kuhn Rd.
Layton NJ 07851   (201) 948-5200

Peters Valley offers two- to eight-day woodworking workshops in June, July, and August. The related Peters Valley Craft Fair is now well over two decades old and is open to all original fine contemporary and traditional craft media, plus photography. Workshop room and board costs depend on length of stay, starting at $55 for the two-day, and going to $410 for the ten-day. Likewise, tuition per course varies, with tuition for John Wilson's Shaker oval boxes course, two days long, only $135, plus a $35 materials fee and a $15 membership fee (the membership fee exists for all courses). A course on making an acoustic guitar lasts eight days, with a tuition of $305 and a materials fee of $400. The course list seems interesting and well thought out, and if the other craftsmen and women are of the quality of John Wilson, certainly the expertise for fine teaching is there. Literature is free.

DEPT. OF FORESTRY AND NATURAL RESOURCES

Purdue University
West Lafayette IN 47907-1159   (317) 494-3590
Daniel L. Cassens, Professor of Wood Products

Purdue offers a whole bunch of finishing seminars, lumber grading, workplace efficiency, wood machining, wood manufacturing, and other wood and woodworking courses that are sometimes of interest for the hobby woodworker and always of interest to the pro. Give them a call or drop a note to get information on dates and places of various courses. Many of the courses for industrial types might be taken for overall content. It's kind of nice to know what the pros think of water-based poly finishes and HVLP (high volume, low pressure) spray application systems, particularly now that the price of hobby units has started dropping into a rational range. There are other subjects that will also match up. If you live within swing distance of Indiana or Michigan (many of the courses are given in cooperation with Michigan State), you may be interested.

ROCKINGHAM COMMUNITY COLLEGE

P.O. Box 38
Wentworth NC 27375   (919) 342-4261

The RCC fine and creative woodworking program is a two-year, daytime, full-time degree program. Scholarships and other aid are offered. In-state tuition is $11.50 per credit hour at this time, but out-of-state hours go for $107.50 each. Courses are offered in the basics, woods and their properties, shop operation and management, chair construction, furniture construction, fixtures, jigs and forms, and many other options.

SCHOOL OF CLASSICAL WOODCARVING

10 Liberty Ship Way
Sausalito CA 94965

This school offers one-, two-, and twelve-week courses in wood carving and stone carving, for furniture and architecture. Write for information on costs and starting dates.

JOHN WILSON

500 E. Broadway Hwy.
Charlotte MI 48813   (517) 543-5325

John is the modern day torchbearer for Shaker oval boxes and offers everything from instruction sheets to the supplies to make the boxes (see listing on page 75). He gives workshops at specific intervals during the year, at varied places, so you don't always have to be in Michigan to learn to make oval boxes. Give him a call, or drop a note, to check prices of current literature and workshops.

WOODENBOAT SCHOOL

P.O. Box 78
Brooklin ME 04616   (207) 359-4651

If your interests cover any part of woodworking that is involved with water, get the course catalog for this school, run from the same complex near Brooklin, Maine, that WoodenBoat Store, *WoodenBoat* magazine, and *Professional Boatbuilder* call home. I have been there once and was impressed with the abiding interest, bordering strongly on love, that most of the people who work there have for the activity and their various interests that relate to that activity. The place is gorgeous, with old buildings put to what are now traditional uses. If you are interested in woodworking as it bears on making boats, the courses cover fundamentals of boatbuilding, lofting, and building various small wooden boats (the catalog I am looking at offers courses in a 16' harbor skiff, The Wee Lassie [featherweight canoe], Haven 12½, DK-14 kayak, Nutshell Pram from a kit, Maine guide canoe, dory skiff, Norwegian sailing pram, 12' fisherman's skiff, and a snipe). In addition, there are courses in rigging, seasmanship, navigation, sail, kayaking, marine mechanics and electrics, astronomy, marine painting and varnishing, basic woodworking for boatbuilding, joinery, and much else. Courses vary a bit in price, but the most costly is $745 for a two-week course (Building the Haven 12½), and most others are $450 or $420. Some courses have a materials cost, and some offer a raffle for the boat built by students. The maximum number of students in most courses at one time is ten. There is much more to tell, but let them do it. Drop a line, or give them a call and ask for the course catalog.

WoodenBoat School students get passing grades and a chance to use their creations.

Boat plans to project layout knowledge are essential to successful work. Courtesy of WoodenBoat School.

Boat framing must be light but extremely sturdy.
Courtesy of WoodenBoat School.

WORCESTER CENTER FOR CRAFTS

25 Sagamore Rd.
Worcester MA 01605   (508) 753-8183

Call or write for the Professional Crafts catalog, describing two-year programs in woodworking and other crafts.

YESTERMORROW INC.

Box 344
Warren VT 05674   (802) 496-5545

Yestermorrow offers coordinated courses, with students learning design from designers and application from applicators. As an example, architects teach building design and contractors teach construction. Over the years, the original concept has been applied to a growing number of courses, now including a decently wide range of building related trades and professions, including cabinetmaking, CAD

training, shop assembly, and other areas. Woodworking curriculum courses are one week long, geared to three levels of ability. Courses such as Cabinetry I, II, and II start you at the beginning and may be stacked (II starts the day after I ends, if you want, but may also be taken later, with no delay moving into level III). Tuition and room and board for a week-long course are currently $1,025 (that includes breakfast, brown bag lunches, and dinners). Faculty lists appear to emphasize design, though there is obviously a great deal of hands-on experience as well. For example, Dick Roberge has a bachelor's degree in fine arts, but runs his own cabinetmaking and woodworking shop and has studied with Tage Frid. John Connell founded the school in 1980; he holds a master's in architecture, is a licensed architect, and teaches at Yale's architecture school. Sounds very interesting.

Plans and Kits

ACCENT SOUTHWEST

P.O. Box 35277
Albuquerque NM 87176

Santa Fe-style furniture plans are offered in the $3.00 Accents Southwest furniture catalog. The plans are said to be well thought out, with start-to-finish instructions. The catalog shows a good array of useful furniture pieces, including a corner curio cabinet, a choice of dining table shapes, and a rocking chair. Along the way, there are also plans for a sofa and lounge chair, a sideboard, and dressers. Prices for plans range from $5.00 for a wall mirror to $20.00 for the sideboard.

ACCENTS IN PINE

Box 7387
Gonic NH 03867

In the 1,000+ patterns Accents in Pine offers, you will find a package of rack and stand plans, including patterns for a ski rack, coat racks, quilt and blanket stands, and others. Down the pages a bit, one of the Pro-Paks offers three children's stools. The Pro-Paks are intended as easy-to-make projects for commercial craftsmen, and feature fewer projects than most packs. Packages run $8.00 each, and usually include at least half a dozen — often more, and sometimes many more — plans (set #16 has eight whirligigs; set #14 has ten bird feeders; set #19 presents more than thirty Christmas decorations and centerpieces). Patterns, if the sample (moosehead clothes rack) sent to me is true of all, are well done, in blueprint format, and easy to read. Each pattern has tips from James C. Olds, Jr., including tips on retailing your results. The catalog is $1.00.

THE AMERICAN COASTER

7106 Lake Rd.
Montrose MI 48457

Plans for wood coaster wagons, sled wagons, and wood wheelbarrows. Plans are $12.95 each, $21.95 for two, or $29.95 for all three, including shipping and handling. A brochure of plans and parts kits is available for $1.00.

AMERICAN PLYWOOD ASSOCIATION

P.O. Box 11700
Tacoma WA 98411-0700   (206) 565-6600

The APA Handy Plan catalog is $2.00. It lists and shows a wide variety of projects built primarily — naturally enough — of plywood in one form or another. The APA also offers many low cost booklets, brochures, and tech sheets that are of great help when larger projects loom, and plywood in large amounts and numbers of types must be bought. Ask about a listing of such technical bulletins.

AMERICAN WORKSHOP SERIES

4642 Wilkens Ave.
Suite 420   (410) 536-5128
Baltimore MD 21229   FAX: (410) 247-8813

The American Workshop Series Preindustrial Arts early country furniture plans catalog (no price listed) offers patterns that look more than vaguely familiar to me from the many years I spent in New York's Hudson River Valley. Many of the patterns are similar to pieces I saw at that time, and the plan included with the information package Jack Bucheimer provided closely resembles blanket chests I have seen and used. The plan is a black line (diazo process) drawing of an actual piece; construction directions are detailed and seem excellent. The actual piece is presented as coming from south central Pennsylvania sometime between 1820 and 1840, while the similar piece I saw was ensconced in a house built around 1839, in Clinton, NY (Duchess County), an area of Dutch settlement. (Most of the Hudson River, up to and past Albany, NY, was thoroughly settled by the

This easy to build desk is an American Plywood Association project.

Dutch long before the English arrived; anyone in the area of the Stockade, in Schenectady, NY, can check the large number of houses built in the late 1600s. By this time, it has probably been all prissed up, but when I worked there, it was genuine and lovely, with much of it still authentic and without the nonsensical revisionist addenda one finds today.) Dovetail patterns in the chest, to retain authenticity, may have to be hand cut, but might also be done on a Leigh or Porter-Cable Omni dovetail jig, allowing for changes in one or the other set. (Tail angles change as one tail is ½" across the base, with a top width of ⅛", while the other set is ⅜" across the base with a ⅛" top width. The space between the dovetails is different too.)

Most of the plans from the American Workshop Series are not for novices, though with care, I think all but the rawest novice might follow the plan. Plans include the blanket/dower chest, jelly cupboard, paneled-back settle, New England farm table, six-board blanket chest, and others. Plan prices range from $6.00 for a five-board footstool diagram to $14.00 for the hooded paneled back settle.

AMERICANA DESIGNS

3134 Grayland Ave.
Richmond VA 23221

Americana Designs offers more than a hundred original gingerbread patterns for mantels, shelves, screen doors, and gate designs. The catalog is $3.00.

ANNE'S CALICO CAT ORIGINALS

Box 1004
Oakdale CA 95361

For $1.00, Anne Engert will send a catalog of crafting patterns and cutouts, all of cats. From the color photos Anne sent, the patterns are attractive and the cuts very nicely done. The CAT-alog, as Anne calls it, brings with it a $2.00 off coupon for your first order. She will also supply a sample plan packet for $3.00, the plan to be one of her choice.

ARMOR

Box 445   (800) 292-8296
East Northport NY 11731   (516) 462-6228
                                              FAX: (516) 462-5793

John Capotosto writes that, for my readers, he is reducing the standard $1.00 catalog price to zero. That was the second nice surprise in John's package. The 72-page catalog is not just of plans, but contains many small tools, finishes, furniture trim, hardware, and other items, plus four pages of books. Clock plans range from a 77" Washington Hall Clock to a simple outline-cut cowboy boot clock. John also offers a classic roll-top desk plan (with or without his parts

kit), cheval mirror, gun cabinets, dry sinks, workbenches, tea carts, cradles, desks, children's outdoor furniture, billiard tables, table soccer plans, lamp plans, rocking horses, toys, vehicles, doll houses (including kits), and more. Many of the plans are developments for John's articles in top do-it-yourself and craft magazines over the years and are well worth reviewing. The catalog is a must see.

ASHLAND BARNS

990-WBS Butlercreek
Ashland OR 97520   (503) 488-1541

The eighty-two barn and mini-barn plans offered in Ashland's $5.00 catalog (refunded with plans order) are supplemented by a second catalog at $2.00 (again, refunded with order), offering plans for weather vanes and signs, adorned with "critters" as Jay Wallace puts it. The cuts of signs, weather vanes, and a barn show interesting design features, so if projects along these lines are in your area of interest, give Jay a call or drop him a note requesting the catalogs.

THE BERRY BASKET

P.O. Box 925
Centralia WA 98531   (206) 736-7020

The Berry Basket is the only company I have seen listing collapsible basket patterns. Drop a note or give a call for further information.

BRYANT HOUSE

8295 Ison Rd.
Atlanta GA 30350

Hardwood furniture kits in traditional designs, with easy construction and finishing are the products of Bryant House. Write for further information.

CALIFORNIA REDWOOD ASSOCIATION

405 Enfrente Dr., Suite 200
Novato CA 94949   (415) 382-0662

For a wide range of literature on types and uses of redwood lumber, the California Redwood Association can't be beat. The emphasis is on outdoor use, as one might expect, though I have found redwood makes an interesting material for large and small indoor projects as well. (I built two redwood bookshelves some time ago. They continue to stand in my dining room, where their appearance often draws comments because redwood is seldom used for such projects. Most indoor redwood projects are architectural, covering uses such as wall paneling and molding.) The Association's literature list offers everything from a Design-

This is a redwood planter. Courtesy of California Redwood Association.

A-Deck plans kit to nail use information. Exterior and interior finishes are covered in large brochures, and there are pamphlets on the industry and its harvesting methods and the environmental impact of using redwood. I suggest giving the Association a call or dropping them a note to request the literature list, at which time you can ask about shipping costs added to literature prices on the list.

CHRIOLYN DESIGNS

P.O. Box 531056
Orlando FL 32853-1056

Chriolyn presents a line of children's furniture plans, specializing in toy boxes, plus a complete line of home furniture. The catalog is $2.00.

CLARK CRAFT

16 Aqua Lane   (716) 873-2640
Tonawanda NY 14150   FAX: (716) 873-2651

Clark Craft presents a catalog of boat kits and plans, for a non-refundable $5.00, first class mail; $2.50 for bulk mail. The catalog order includes a separate boatbuilding supply catalog that includes books, more plans, many laminating and finishing tools and supplies, boat nails and screws (silicon bronze is the featured material), fiberglass cloth,

Redwood provides the means to carry out many project ideas, as in this bedroom. Courtesy of California Redwood Association.

matt, woven roving and tape, and resins, with detailed instructions for the use of epoxy. The boat plan and kit catalog takes you from a canoe and a six-foot dinghy on up to a Roberts 64 sailboat. Along the way, there are plans for kayaks, hovercraft, tunnel hull runabouts, racers, houseboats, and even a 70' steel hull cruiser. Prices of plans and patterns start at $20 and rise to $695 for the 70 steel hull cruiser, jumping to $749 for the Roberts 64. Study prints are available at far lower cost ($30 for the Roberts 64, $20 for the steel 70 footer). Boat kits start at $225 for the little dinghy and scamper up to $6,650 for a Crown Cruiser 26'. Larger boats, and many not so large, are available only as plans kits, but some have frame, hull, and fastening kits available too.

CONSTANTINE'S

2050 Eastchester Rd.
Bronx NY 10461   (800) 223-8087

Constantine's has been in business since 1812, in one form or another (not always mail order, and today, not totally mail order with two retail outlets). In addition to many pages of books, there are two pages of plans for projects from a mounted kaleidoscope to a French Colonial cradle, with others being rod and gun cabinets, a 15th century wooden clock, doll houses, rocking horses, tool boxes, tea carts, and many others. Almost any aspect of woodworking with an emphasis on veneers is to be found in the full-color catalog. Send $1.00 and go on the catalog list for two years. Constantine's carries many books, videos, and unusual finishing supplies.

CORNERSTONE DESIGNS

6346-65 Lantana Rd.
Suite 10-CS
Lake Worth FL 33463   (407) 439-1570

Cornerstone Designs is a fairly new company, offering a wide range of furniture plans, with toy plans expected to be offered by the time this book is in print. The $2.00 for Cornerstone's catalog is refundable with the first order. The catalog presents some interesting and unusual desk designs, including a two-post desk that looks as if it is interesting both to build and to use. Several of the other projects also offer unique features. Plans are 18" x 24" in blueprint style.

CRAFT PATTERNS

3545 Stern Ave.   Customer service: (800) 747-1429
St. Charles, IL 60174   (708) 584-3334

Craft Patterns offers either a $3.95 catalog of many patterns or free seasonal brochures of lesser numbers of plans. The company has been in business since 1940 and is now run by a second generation. The retail packaging of the *Project-of-*

the-Week is new, and there are two plans in each package. I've checked over potting bench and workbench plans (same package) and find them nicely designed and drawn. The detail is excllent, and there should be no difficulty in building the projects. I suggest asking for the brochures first to see if the project types appeal, but there is a wide enough variety for almost anyone, from small barns and large garages to cradles and birdhouses.

CRAFTER'S MART

Box 2342
Greeley CO 80632   (800) 999-3445

Musical wooden Ferris wheel parts and plans are included in Crafter's Mart's $2.00 catalog.

ARCH DAVIS DESIGN

P.O. Box 119
Morrill ME 04952   (207) 342-4055

Arch forced me to work extra by sending me his book on making raised panels on a table saw (*The Raised Panel Book*, $9.95 plus $2.00 shipping) and a booklet on knowing wood moisture content ($2.00, postage and handling included). He sells plans for a lobster boat and a sailboat and is aiming to have three more plan packages ready shortly. Drop a note for his price list. The plans, from which he sent me a couple of sheets, are nicely done.

DECORATIVE WOODCRAFTS

6060 Spine Rd.
P.O. Box 54696
Boulder CO 80323-4696

This magazine is aimed at those of you who are interested in painting and otherwise decorating your woodworking projects. There are at least a dozen projects in each issue, with removable full-size patterns for some. Bi-monthly, it costs $19.97 a year.

DIXIE GUN WORKS

P.O. Box 130
Union City TN 38261   (901) 885-0700

The Dixie Gun Works presents a huge 600-page catalog ($4.00) including muzzle-loading gun kits.

FAMILY HANDYMAN PLAN SERVICE

P.O. Box 695
Stillwater MN 55083

Send a stamped, self-addressed envelope for a list of furniture plans.

FOREST ST. DESIGNS

538 Holiday Dr.
Brigham City UT 84302

Attaché case, coffeetable/stereo cabinet, and world map plans (each continent in a different veneer) are available ($10.95 for each of the first two, $8.95 for the map, $25.95 for the package, including shipping and a free catalog).

FROG TOOL COMPANY

P.O. Box 8325
Chicago IL 60661   (312) 648-1270

Many, many books (including most of my woodworking books), patterns for wood cutouts, and a great many project plans. The aim here is absolute top quality tools and plans. Catalog is $5.00.

FURNITURE DESIGNS, INC.

1827 Elmdale Ave.
Glenview IL 60025   (708) 657-7526

Interesting furniture plans, including library chair-steps, are the forte of Furniture Designs, Inc. Their catalog is $3.00 and lists more than two hundred full-size furniture plans over a wide range that even includes rocking horses.

GATTO PLAN SUPPLY

Box 1568, R.D. 1
Hamburg PA 19526

Daniel Gatto's plans are wheeled models of superb appearance, with great detail. Included are a wood block backhoe/front end loader, a farm tractor, a 1930 Ford Model A Roadster (including its sixteen-spoke wheels), an eighty-part pickup truck, right down to an opening tailgate, a fifty-piece '57 replica car that looks a lot like a '57 Chevy, and a Monster Truck that thoroughly demonstrates the big wheel craze that has been going on for years, including four shock absorbers per wheel, and K.C. lights. Many plans include options, and plan prices range from $4.95 to $7.95. Projects are readily built from scrap wood and dowels. The brochure is $.75.

GILLIOM MANUFACTURING, INC.

P.O. Box 1018
St. Charles MO 63302   (314) 724-1812

If you have any desire to make your own power tools, kits from Gilliom may be the incentive you need to get started. The list includes a 12" bandsaw, an 18" bandsaw, a 10" tilt arbor table saw, a lathe and drill press combination, a 9" tilt table table saw, a 6" belt sander, a spindle shaper, and a

circular saw table, at $7.50 each or $25.00 for the package of eight plans. The descriptive brochure is $2.00, and kits are available to help build the tools.

HAPPY BEAVER WOODWORKERS

P.O. Box 5142
Rosewood OR 97470

Not only do the Happy Beavers offer butterfly patterns (brochure $1.00), but they have the completed puzzles for butterflies, cows, train engines, and a slew of other wood puzzles and devices. The finished puzzles are sanded and finished with a non-toxic sealer before acrylic paints are laid on. Then a top coat goes on to protect the painted finish. Puzzles range in price from $5.00 to $18.00, with butterflies going from $10.00 to $15.00.

Some of the Happy Beaver line of patterns and cut-outs.

JAPAN WOODWORKER

1731 Clement
Alameda CA 94501   (800) 537-7820

Not only are there extensive lines of Japanese woodworking tools in this catalog (two-year subscription for $1.50), but the book lines for Japanese woodworking concepts are extensive. The company is the original importer of Japanese woodworking tools and a principal supplier today. (See listing on page 95.)

LEICHTUNG WORKSHOPS

4944 Commerce Parkway   (800) 237-5907
Cleveland OH 44128   (216) 464-6764

Leichtung offers a variety of unusual tools, plus many plans and woodworking supplies in their free catalog. The catalog is digest size, but runs over 90 pages, and presents plans,

LL Enterprises round picnic table and arched benches.

some kits (varying with the seasons, but often small boxes and clocks, ships, dollhouses), and parts to help in building some of the plan items. (See listing on page 97.)

LL ENTERPRISES

Box 908
Cornville AZ 86325

One of LL Enterprises more popular plans is for a round picnic table with arched, detached benches. The plans make what could be a complex job seem easy. The catalog, which costs $1.00, offers many more plans for outdoor and indoor furniture with specific projects for children and adults, including a swinging cradle, loveseats, chaise lounges, patio rockers, toy chest, step stool, TV-VCR-game cart, end tables, and more. If all plans live up to the set A.J. Lombardi sent (the round picnic table), you will have no trouble making these projects.

MASTERCRAFT PLANS WEST

P.O. Box 625
Redmond WA 98073

Mastercraft Plans offers full-size patterns for gifts and novelties, including thirty birdhouse and feeder patterns, a garden furniture packet with sixteen lawn chair plans, plus a slew of tables, a swing, lounge, settee, and other items.

Other packets include shelves, jig saw projects, garden windmills, more garden projects, a gift and novelty pack, a variety pack (ranges from a magazine basket to a picnic table, and includes a trellis, hanging shelves, and about five dozen other plans), a country crafts packet, and a couple more types. Patterns are ready to cut or trace. Plan packages are $8.00 each, including first class return mail. Send an SASE for the list.

MCCRAFTS

2632 Starnes Rd.
Charlotte NC 28214

Offering ten easy-to-make plans for $12.00, McCrafts calls the vehicles Exec Toys. Designed for easy fabrication with just a bandsaw and a drill.

MEISEL HARDWARE SPECIALTIES

P.O. Box 70
Mound MN 55364-0070   (800) 441-9870

Paul Meisel offers a wide variety of plans, with projects shown in update catalogs keyed to seasons. (Once you get on the list, you can expect to look at Christmas projects in the catalog that arrives around the end of July. This allows the woodworker to work up Christmas [Halloween and Thanksgiving projects are in the same catalog] projects for sale or for gifts, well in advance of the season). Paul's specialties in the plan area are often — far from always, though — cut-out patterns for use as lawn ornaments. He also offers simple nativity plans and enough yard ornament plans to literally cover a huge lawn. Plans are offered as just plans, or as combinations of plans and hardware kits. You may also buy the hardware — sleigh bells, wind streamer material (for Santa's beard) — separately. The larger Meisel Hardware Specialties catalogs offer such items as a slingshot drag racer, powered by a rubber band, and rocking horse plans that are really fine (the rocking horse can be bought in a number of styles, including with rockers already cut). The hardware sampler catalog I recently received offers white porcelain knobs, Colonial hinges, wood ball knobs, clock faces, and much more specialty material. Paul will supply *Woodworker's Source Book* readers with a free catalog subscription.

BOB MEYER

7347 Hwy. 247 NE
Elgin MN 55932   (507) 876-2482

This is a case where I have to hope my editors can find space for all three of the clock designs Bob produces. One uses a 48" main gear and a 36" escarpment gear — of wood! Another plan, for a wooden geared standing clock, uses wood and bathroom tubing (polished aluminum) for a clock that is 87" tall. The third is a wooden geared wall clock 24" long. All gears on the latter are cut from ¾" hardwood veneer plywood, as are those in the other clocks, and may be cut with a jigsaw. Clock plans range from $15.00 for the wall clock to $25.00 for the standing clock to $40.00 for the monster. Except for the big clock plans, Bob discounts the plans when you buy more than one.

Bob Meyer's monster 4' diameter clock gear.

This is Bob Meyer's wood geared wall clock.

*Bob Meyer's wood geared standing clock, with a 15"
diameter wooden gear.*

MINDY'S PUZZLES

Box 176
Elk City ID 83525　　　　　　　(208) 842-2265

For $5.00 plus $1.25 postage, Mindy Wiebush will ship you
more than twenty puzzle patterns, in sizes ranging from 6"
x 9" to 10" x 15", with the resulting puzzles designed to suit
skill levels from two years to over five years (not for construction, but for puzzle assembly). A sheet of carbon paper is
provided for tracing patterns onto wood, and a six-page tip
sheet makes the already simple scroll and bandsaw patterns
even simpler and safer to do right. Mindy also sends along
a few critter patterns to help reduce scrap wood buildup
(kids really do love these simple items) and offers, for an
additional $4.50 including shipping, fifty other animal
patterns. Ask for the Critter Packet.

MUSICMAKER'S KITS, INC.

423 South Main　　　　　　　(800) 432-KITS
Stillwater MN 55082　　　　　　(612) 439-9120

Jerry Brown seems to offer about every type of acoustic
instrument kit that might be of interest. The kit list includes
hammer dulcimers, mountain dulcimers, harps, banjos,
guitars, mountain mandolins, steel string guitar (six- or
twelve-string), an item called a hurdy-gurdy, string bass,
panpipes, wooden fife, garden harp, window harp, door
harps, a wooden drum, thumb piano, full-sized harps, and
a series of special order kits that include a Martin classical
guitar, a violin, a small bagpipe, and even a spinet harpsichord. In addition, Jerry has bits and pieces for scratch
builders, including tuning pins, fret scale graph, eyelets, and
much more. To work from plans, get one of his door harp
or guitar plans, or any of a couple dozen other plans for
everything from a hammer dulcimer to a psaltery. (Actually,
from a banjo to a violin, if we stay alphabetical.) Woods,
dyes, finishes, and clamps are also offered.

PINECRAFT PATTERNS

P.O. Box 13186
Green Bay WI 54307-3186

Lawn ornaments, shelves, bird houses, porch swings, picnic
tables, and cabinets make up the forty-plus plans in Pinecraft's
$6.95 package (including shipping and handling).

PLEASURE CRAFTS

Route 2, Box 1485
Mannford OK 74044

Danny Cheney of Pleasure Crafts produces full-sized traceable patterns for balancing toys and other wooden mechanical toys and usable folk art items. The packages of plans,
described in free brochures, present a total of over 135
patterns. Each book of patterns is $10.00, or all three are

$27.00, postpaid. Patterns include a mass of toys that are difficult to describe, accurately and in terms of apparent actions, but there is a girl on parallel bars, a cowboy with a lariat, a rocking clown, a fisherman catching a fish, a swinging bear, a card-showing magician, a rope-jumping pair, climbing clowns, spice racks, memo holders, coat hangers, and many, many more. Write for the brochures.

QUAKER STATE WOODWORKING SUPPLY

Airport Industries Bldg. #2
RD 9, Box 9386
Reading PA 19605

Quaker State Woodworking Supply offers plans, tools, accessories, and a growing catalog/newsletter, currently in the 16-page range. Drop a card to be added to the list for their monthly publication.

RJS CUSTOM WOODWORKING

P.O. Box 12354
Kansas City KS 66112

My listing for RJS started out noting they had toy carousel plans, but when I received their most recent catalog (printed

Get an adjustable footstool plan at RJS Custom Woodworking.

The puzzle plan is from RJS Custom Woodworking.

on recycled paper, with a request that it be recycled after a new catalog arrives), I noted that plans, even excellent full-sized carousel plans and plans for dream car plaques (if your dream car is a Ferrari or a Rolls), are only a part of the line. See listing on page 104 for more information.

SPECIALTY FURNITURE DESIGNS OF MICHIGAN

797 W. Remus Rd.
Mt. Pleasant MI 48858

Specialty Furniture Designs has six different planter designs, including a planter bench combination, many picnic table plans, and other plans using nominal 2" materials. The color catalog is $2.00.

STEWART-MACDONALD

Box 900   (800) 848-2273
Athens OH 45701   FAX: (614) 593-7922

The 104-page free catalog offers plans for a number of instruments: guitar (solid and acoustic bodies), mandolin, and banjo. In addition, Stewart-MacDonald carries many odd tools and supplies (to me, with a total lack of experience in this area of woodworking), including such products as fret tang nippers, three-corner fret files, bridge pin hole reamers, and similar items, which are at the least exotically named. Also offered are video courses in guitar repair, pearl

inlay techniques, gluing secrets, servicing a tube amp, guitar finishing, and more. To add to the line of information, Stewart-MacDonald carries many tools other than those already mentioned, and goes on to carry a lot of familiar supplies (Hydrocote and Behlen finishes, HVLP spray finish outfits, dial calipers, and so on) amongst the bending irons, spool clamps, bridge clamps, bridge saddle routing jigs, and much more. They also carry the first actual vacuum tubes for amplifiers that I've seen in longer than I care to think about, as well as a couple of dulcimer kits that look interesting and not too difficult to build.

SUN DESIGNS

173 E. Wisconsin Ave.   (414) 567-4255
Oconomowoc WI 53066   FAX: (414) 567-4173

Sun Designs is a small company producing design books and construction plans for yard and other projects. Strom Toys is considered a classic of toy design and making and is one of the products from Sun. Janet Strombeck kindly sent along blueprints for the Victoria, a truly lovely sleigh, and a copy of *Timeless Toys In Wood* for me to examine. If I still lived in an area with decent amounts of winter weather — snow, for example — I would quickly build the Victoria, and go further and produce the Bunker Hill sled. Even without a local winter wonderland, I find plenty of toy plans. The engine and coal car in *Timeless Toys* are an example, large enough to provide riding models for small

The whimsical bridge and duck house are also from Sun Designs.

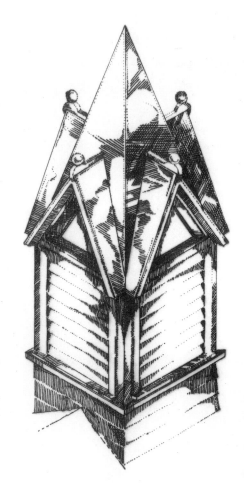

Sun Designs offers large and small plans. We saw some small plans earlier, and these cupolas are intermediate size.

children, with enough accessories and other cars to keep a woodworking parent or grandparent busy for a long time.

The designs shown in *Gazebos and Other Garden Structures* will keep many a woodworker or carpenter employed for an even longer period. *Gazebos* is an idea book, with plans for the most part available as extra attractions at varying prices (birdhouse or feeder plans, for example, are about $5.95 each; buy more, get a discount per plan; gazebo plans are $24.95 each). You'll see drawings of some of the plans, many of which are ornate and correspondingly difficult to build. Others are less ornate and less difficult to erect. The four-color brochure is $.50. Sun Designs also mail orders accessory packages for their toy designs.

TAUNTON PRESS

63 S. Main St.
Box 355
Newtown CT 06470   (203) 426-8171

This publisher offers a line of videos, books, a top woodworking magazine (*Fine Woodworking*), and a free catalog.

TIMBERS COUNTRY STORE

P.O. Box 897
Wheatley ONT   (819) 825-7480
Canada N0P 2P0   FAX: (819) 825-3780

I first heard of Timbers Country Store as a source for doll house parts and plans, and a single page certainly proves that to be the case, with cedar shakes, siding, and a line of windows and doors that looks very interesting. They have a special order setup and catalog that provide much more. Added to the doll house plans and parts there are game plans and parts and many, many kinds of plans for furniture, toys, and other items. Timbers also sells hardware, small tools, clock kits, accessories for just about anything, including lamp kits, books, wood parts, musical movements, and whirligig parts. The catalog is free. It's difficult to judge Canadian prices from the U.S. because I don't keep track of exchange rates, but I imagine your bank, or Timbers Country Store, can give any U.S. customers an angle on the rates.

TOY TRUCKS UNLIMITED

P.O. Box 15624
Rochester NY 14615

Send an SASE for a list of toy plans that includes many trucks.

TOYS AND JOYS

Box 628
Lyndon WA 98264

The $1.00 Toys and Joys catalog expands on a list of patterns, wheels, pegs, dowels, and kits with the aim being primarily wooden vehicles that are extremely nicely detailed.

TREND-LINES

375 Beacham St.   Catalog request number:
Chelsea MA 02150   (800) 366-6966

Trend-Lines is a discount mail order house, offering many plans and project books, plus general woodworking books, in their free catalog presenting more than 3,000 brand-name products, including power tools and accessories, hand tools, screws, hardware, and wood parts. Stan Black always has interesting plans listed, often some new tools, and produces a catalog that packs a lot of interest for woodworkers. Complete satisfaction guaranteed.

TURNCRAFT

P.O. Box 100
Mound MN 55364-0100   (800) 544-1711

This is a new addition to the lineup of mail order companies, specializing in different and unusual, as well as traditional, clock parts and clock plans. (See listing on page 111.) Drop a line and request the catalog if you're at all interested in making reasonably simple clocks.

WESTERN WOOD PRODUCTS ASSOCIATION

Yeon Building
522 S.W. Fifth Ave.
Portland OR 97204-2122

WWPA presents technical information on the species of wood their association emphasizes (Douglas fir, hem-fir, Engelmann spruce, Idaho white pine, lodgepole pine, sugar pine, Ponderosa pine, Western larch, Western cedars, and incense cedar), plus a good series of large and small plans at low cost. I'm looking at a plan for kid-sized storage modules now, their #62: it is easy to build and uses standard lumber sizes. Plan #61 is a mobile workbench that looks no harder to build. Drop a note asking for the current literature list or catalog of plans. The list is too long to reproduce here but contains a good variety of plans that will almost certainly have one of interest to you.

WILLIAMS TOOL & HARDWARE SUPPLY

2017 White Settlement Rd.
Fort Worth TX 76107   (800) 338-6668

Mail order plans, large and small, books on a wide variety of woodworking subjects, general woodworking tools and supplies, including Amana router bits, Incra system jigs and rigs, Porter-Cable, Dremel, Ryobi, Makita, Bosch, Delta, and Hitachi power tools, ready-to-assemble drawers, roller stands, Freud and Delta blades, sanding drums, abrasive accessories, wood parts, and Olson scroll saw blades. Catalog is free.

WINFIELD COLLECTION

1450 Torrey Rd.
Fenton MI 48430-3310   (313) 629-7712

I've got three of the Winfield Collection catalogs in front of me, with a huge assortment of country woodcraft patterns listed and illustrated. The $1.00 catalog subscription gives you a good chance at finding something you like over time. Projects, from birdhouses to stands and other furniture and including lawn ornaments and toys, are designed to be quickly and easily made, which adds to fun and makes for a good chance of profit if you're going to do crafts as more than a hobby. Furniture projects, which are designed to use pine or similar low cost woods (as are all the projects), include a corner country cupboard, a pie safe, a deacon's bench, a child's rocking chair, a hall table, a quilt rack, and many others. Patterns are full-sized, set to be traced onto the wood, cut out, and assembled. Pattern prices start at $1.00 and go up to $11.50, with most in the $5.00 area. Here's a personal tip on traceable patterns: do *not* try to do the tracing completely freehand. Use straight edges and French curves as needed to stabilize your tracing, so lines will be cleaner and easier to cut accurately.

WOOD MOULDING & MILLWORK
PRODUCERS ASSN.

Box 25278
Portland OR 97225   (503) 292-9288

The WMMPA offers a book with five hundred wood moulding projects for $5.50. Other consumer literature tells how to work with wood mouldings (the association retains the British spelling), describes the trip from tree to trim, and shows how to remodel homes with wood moulding. Consumer literature prices range from $.50 to the above $5.50, and the brochure describing the literature is free.

WOOD-MET SERVICES

3314 Shoff Circle
Peoria IL 61604   (309) 637-4667

Wood-Met has passed its tenth anniversary, and Norwood Snowden sent me a pile of material to show how useful the seven hundred or so plans that are included in his $1.00 (refundable) catalog actually are. No argument there, with over eighty attachments for lathes, drill presses, and routers. The preponderance of Wood-Met Services plans tends to lean to the metal working, but there are more than enough woodworking tool and accessory plans to make the catalog worthwhile. Shop equipment, portable power tools, and accessories such as a mobile wood lathe tool holder are very useful. Plans are small scale but clear and nicely dimensioned. Instructions are clear. Snowden spent forty-one years with Caterpillar design, research, and development before retiring and starting Wood-Met.

WOODARTIST

Box 31564
Charleston SC 29417

Send an SASE for a list of plans for antique birdhouses.

WOODCRAFTS BY JOHN DALY

Rt 10, Box 708
Lake City FL 32055

John Daly presents five bandsaw toy car plans for $8.00 (all five), or $2.00 each. The patterns cover a pickup, a Jeep, a 1957 Chevy, a 1957 Corvette, and a 1935 Auburn. The patterns are not elegant, but the drawings are clear, and the instructions concise and easy to follow. The cars are designed to be bandsawed from 2x4 stock, and John notes that the patterns become reusable if you transfer them to cardboard. I will make a slightly different suggestion: transfer the patterns to ¼" lauan plywood, and cut the patterns on the bandsaw. It's easier to get the curves right, and the patterns are then about 5,000 times more durable. Send a stamped self-addressed envelope for the free brochure describing the patterns.

WOODEN MEMORIES

Route 1, Box 87
Bear Lake PA 16402   (814) 489-3002

Send $1.00 and Wooden Memories will send you a color catalog of plans. Plans include full-sized patterns that need only be traced onto the wood, at which time you may cut out the pattern and paste it onto the wood, after painting.

WOODWORKERS' STORE

21801 Industrial Blvd.   (612) 428-2199
Rogers MN 55374-9514   FAX: (612) 428-8668

The Woodworkers' Store carries a wide line of plans, books, small power tools, hand tools, woods, finishes, jigs, kits, and a very wide line of hardware, including many porcelain parts, oak and birch carvings, and even briefcase handles in two quality levels (the cheaper is covered in vinyl, the more costly in leather). Plans include doll houses, whirligigs, desks, rocking toys, entertainment centers, tool centers, cedar chest, and a number of cradles. You'll also find a large line of jewelry box, chest and drawer, and general cabinet locks, and plenty of knockdown fasteners. Currently unique is their line of workshop knobs in black plastic or aluminum, in five styles and many more sizes. The knobs make building your own shop jigs a great deal easier, as do some other new kits in the most recent catalog. The Woodworkers' Store is another company that sends smaller update catalogs with some frequency, so your $3.00 buys a great deal of information.

WORKSHOPPE ORIGINALS

P.O. Box 86
Wildomar CA 92595   (714) 678-9503

Plans consist of full-size patterns, typically of flat yard designs: Santa's sleigh, Christmasy street lamp, skiing elf and, to change the season, eighteen vegetable garden markers. Other plan packages include Christmas ornaments and gifts, more yard patterns for year round use, and ideas for converting some of the lawn ornament patterns to other uses. Three single-page brochures are done in glossy full color and present fine color suggestions, as well as a good look at the constructed patterns. The catalog, currently of the three brochures, is growing and is $2.00, refunded on the first order. The one payment enters your name for all succeeding brochures and for the full catalog when it arrives in the near future. Patterns range from $6.50 to $12.00 per package (the $12.00 package is the Toyland Express, a 9½ foot long, four piece Christmas train). Patterns come in a 6" x 11" clear plastic package with a full color cover. Instructions are detailed and include painting guides.

Publications — Books and Magazines

AAVIM

745-A Gaines School Rd.
Athens GA 30605   (706) 543-7557

The American Association for Vocational Instructional Materials is a non-profit developer, publisher, and distributor of instructional videos, books, and other resources, including computer software, for vocational students. Primarily, their customers are schools. On request, they'll send along a copy of their 90-page catalog, with woodworking educational materials described in the industrial education section. There are a lot of videos, with the cheapest being a project video complete with a 22-page booklet. Shopsmith's series of woodworking videos is included in the list and is reasonably priced. Regardless of price, there are a fair number of videos and a couple of programs I'd love to own. Most come under the heading of "Maybe, someday," but you may find desires and wallet power that are stronger than mine. The Agriculture section includes some reasonably priced materials on fence building, while the Construction Trades sections contain a lot of material on larger projects with wood. Tip: Get the manuals and forget the software unless you plan to teach classes.

AMERICAN WOODWORKER

33 E. Minor St.	(800) 666-3111
Emmaus PA 18098	(215) 967-5171

AW is a Rodale Press magazine and comes out six times a year. It is almost six years old and has recently changed from an oversized black-and-white magazine to a standard (8½" x 11") four-color format. It offers tech tips, technique articles, many good project articles, finishing tips, a wood fact column, and its own look at subjects every other woodworking magazine also looks at. Fortunately, the angle at which *AW* looks at woodworking is just off center enough to be interesting in its own right. Projects range from the elegant and moderately difficult to the simple and fun. Tool tests are rational and reasonably accurate, though less exhaustive than those in a few other magazines. Overall, a likable and useful publication with its own personality. Six issues per year for $23.70.

DOVER PUBLICATIONS, INC.

31 East 2nd St.
Mineola NY 11501

Dover's catalog is free and lists many woodworking titles and related titles, from old to new. At one time, Dover published only reprints, but in recent years they've gone to publishing more and more new material, while retaining the lead in publishing old crafts (and other) material. They have books on woodturning, for example, that go back centuries to provide plentiful examples of how it was done, with some help toward getting it done today if you apply some study and thought. Always an interesting and fun research tool, the Dover catalog in recent years has turned more into a series of catalogs on different subjects, plus a full line catalog. Ask for the full line catalog, just in case.

FINE TOOL JOURNAL

P.O. Box 4001	Orders: (800) 248-8114
Pittsford VT 05763	(802) 483-2111

Published as a quarterly, *Fine Tool Journal* is jammed with articles on evaluating modern hand tools, historical perspec-

tives for the collector of tools and methods, how-to articles on tuning old and new tools, book reviews, and much more, including listings of antique, obsolete, and modern tools for sale. One year (four issues) is $20.00 ($25.00 U.S. in Canada).

FINE WOODWORKING

Taunton Press
63 South Main St.
P.O. Box 5506
Newtown CT 06470-9971   (203) 426-8171

Currently at $25.00 per year, *Fine Woodworking* is the exemplar of a magazine for top woodworkers of whatever skill level. Those on a lower level are not going to be able to reproduce many of the projects, of which there are fewer than in other magazines, but they will definitely learn something from each issue. After working through enough of the technique articles in *FW*, nearly anyone will be able to do almost anything. Many, many, many shop tips in each of the six issues per year, plus book and video reviews, a look at upcoming events, letters, tool tests, and so on. Some, too often much, of the material tends to the esoteric, such as an article a few years ago on tensioning a bandsaw blade by tone, something that probably works fine for a few, but is dead useless to those of us who are tone deaf. Lots of ads, lots of copy. Oversized magazine, reasonable price.

INFODEX SERVICES

10609 King Arthurs Court
Richmond VA 23235-3840   (804) 320-4704

David Jordan offers his PC program, a large woodworking index, with a subscription service for updates. The program, INFOWARE, provides (at the time this book is written) a database covering more than 6,500 articles in 290 issues of 11 woodworking magazines. Touch the right key and you can find any of the 1,358 projects and plans or other article or tool test you wish. The eleven magazines include the best, from *American Woodworker* to *Workbench*. The program comes on 5¼" or 3½" disks and needs 2.5 megabytes of hard disk space and DOS 3.3 or higher. Approximately 1,500 articles are being added to the database each year. Free information and prices. Subscription updates are mailed in January and June.

LINDEN PUBLISHING, INC.

3845 N. Blackstone
Fresno CA 93726   (800) 345-4447

Linden is a crafts books publisher, with a list of interesting and unusual reprints and new books, including *The Cooper And His Trade, Contract Joinery, A Treatise On Lathes And*

Turning (originally published in 1868), and *Making Wooden Clock Cases*, a new book. The catalog is free, and you might also request the R. Sorsky catalog of titles. While Linden publishes books on woodworking and similar fields, Sorsky sells, at retail, books in the same fields.

HOW-TO BOOK CLUB

Blue Ridge Summit PA 17294

The How-To Book Club is owned by TAB Books, a subsidiary of McGraw-Hill. They will send details and a book list on request.

MANNY'S WOODWORKER'S PLACE

602 S. Broadway
Lexington KY 40508   (606) 255-5444

Give Manny a call to check on his list of woodworking books and videos. The list is very extensive, Manny's takes most credit cards, and the catalog is $2.00.

POPULAR WOODWORKING

1320 Galaxy Way
Concord CA 94520

A good woodworking magazine running a wide variety of articles with many projects, *Popular Woodworking* is a magazine in transition, going from one of the modest members of the group to one of the showier and stronger members. Recent upsurges in the use of color and trademarked Pull-Out Plans, plus more attention to editing detail, have made *PW* a greater force in woodworking. A recent issue provides a good sample of intent, as it is fairly bursting with project articles (fourteen), plus book reviews, video checks, letters, a tool test article, and a wood type piece plus columns and departments. This publication is in year twelve, and a subscription costs $23.70 (six issues).

PROFESSIONAL BOATBUILDER

P.O. Box 78
Brooklin ME 04616   (207) 359-4651

A part of the WoodenBoat complex, this magazine is aimed at the small professional boatbuilder. It is a controlled circulation bi-monthly that costs $35.95 a year for non-qualified subscribers. It is not of direct interest on a woodworking basis, though some of the most sophisticated woodworking anyone will ever see goes into modern pleasure boats. The issue I have covers light-curing resins (for fiberglass and composite materials), shrink-wrapping boats, choosing batteries, and building replicas, plus a project design for a fold-up table to save room. Over time, there are some truly deep articles on marine finishes, adhesives, and

similar topics, so the magazine is worth a look when available. For those outside the business, it isn't going to come close to being worth the price, though it is very interesting. I now know more about batteries than I will ever need, I'm sure.

SHOP NOTES

Woodsmith Corporation
2200 Grand Ave.
Des Moines IA 50312   (800) 333-5854

This is a new magazine, seeming a bit pricey for length and type, but worth it as time trundles on. Individual issues are $4.95 at present, while a one-year (six issues) subscription is $19.95. As the address shows, it's put out by the folks at Woodsmith, and has something of the same classic feel (same editor, Don Peschke, same publisher, Doug Hicks, and much of the same staff, so that's reasonable). *Shop Notes* does use some four color and more spot color. It isn't pricey except on the basis of bulk: you're getting a no-advertising deal here, so all thirty-two pages is meat. And such meat: one article tells how to build a panel saw, a tool I have been drooling over for years. (Some years ago, R.J. De Cristoforo designed one for either *Popular Science* or *Popular Mechanics*, but that's the only shop-built design I'd seen before. The commercial saws run from about $900 and up, mostly up, while Don Peschke says *Shop Notes* spent about $250 total [not including the saw] for their unit.) Projects, tips, and techniques. I sat here and looked over the two issues on hand, then peeled out the card and ordered a subscription.

R. SORSKY, BOOKSELLER

352 W. Bedford, #105   (800) 345-4447
Fresno CA 93711-6079   FAX: (209) 227-3520

Mail order retailer of woodworking and other craft books. Catalog is free, and the list is extensive and made more interesting by the fact that Sorsky is related to Linden Publishing, a small publishing house for craft books. In the most recent catalog, you might order my *Making Pet Houses, Carriers & Other Projects*, or the 1940 Disston tool catalog, or *Woodworking Machinery: Its Rise, Progress, and Construction, with Hints on the Management of Saw Mills and the Economical Conversion of Lumber*, the 1880 first edition of 362 pages, at $135.00, or any of hundreds of other titles.

STACKPOLE BOOKS

P.O. Box 1831   (800) 732-3669
Harrisburg PA 17105   (717) 234-5041
                                            FAX: (717) 234-1359

Stackpole lists many craft titles in a $3.00 catalog (refundable with first order). Their collection of carving books is

Courtesy of Stackpole Books.

Courtesy of Stackpole Books.

Courtesy of Stackpole Books.

Courtesy of Stackpole Books.

impressive, and their more general woodworking project books are often produced in cooperation with Madrigal Publishers, which also puts out *The Woodworker's Journal*, a top notch woodworking magazine that's been around a long time.

STERLING PUBLISHING COMPANY

387 S. Park Ave.   (212) 532-7160
New York NY 10016   (212) 213-2495

Sterling publishes the widest line of woodworking titles currently available. Call or write and check on catalog prices.

TODAY'S WOODWORKER

P.O. Box 6782
Syracuse NY 13217-9916

Some day I'll figure out how a magazine produced in Rogers, Minnesota is more efficiently mailed from, with lists handled in, Syracuse, New York. Whatever the case, it is a common method today to have the subscription department hundreds or thousands of miles away from the editorial people. At this time, it seems to work, as this sponsored publication (The Woodworker's Store is its parent) booms through its fourth year, presenting very clear plans and tips, all of varying difficulty levels. A single year subscription price of $21.95 is sometimes discounted for new subscribers (currently $18.95) so check before ordering. The magazine is very nicely done, in full color on slick paper, with at least one (two in the issue I'm looking at) well presented and printed full-size plan per issue.

WEEKEND WOODCRAFTS

1320 Galaxy Way
Concord CA 94520

This 1992 startup from EGW Publishing features much of the same staff as *Popular Woodworking* and has a familiar look. There are no shop tips or hints, so the 48-page bimonthly (six issues per year for $21.00) offers a string of easily built projects. There are ten in the issue I'm checking, with everything done in color, and full-size Pull-Out Plans for some projects. Projects are all simple enough or small enough to be built in a single weekend. Well worth a check if your interest is in fast projects, particularly those that might prove salable in craft fairs.

WEEKEND WOODWORKING PROJECTS

1716 Locust St.
Des Moines IA 50336   (800) 678-2666

Subscription price currently is $24.97 for this bimonthly (six issues per year, in January, March, May, July, September, and November) from Meredith Corporation. Featur-

ing half a dozen easy-to-make or small projects in each issue, the magazine has presented a full-size butter churn, a child's rocker, and an hourglass all in a single issue. Using double covers, the staff managed to work in a short tip feature between covers, with other tips (related to included projects) as needed. Nicely done in mostly two or three colors, with a four-color cover, this is another that is well worth a look for those of you interested in small, faster projects.

WOOD

Wood Customer Service
P.O. Box 55050
Boulder CO 80322-5050   (800) 374-9663

One of what has become a multitude of very well done woodworking magazines in recent years, Better Homes & Gardens' *Wood* presents everything from simple projects to complex plans, plus tips, tool tests, tested jigs, shop hints, on through a long list of useful types of articles. Some of the project articles are among the most attractive to be found without overblown extra complexity; that is, the plans can be readily followed by most intermediate woodworkers with patience and time to work things out. Some may even be readily accomplished by lower end intermediate woodworkers, and a few will work for novices. Tool article advice has recently improved. It used to be fact sheet stuff, but now some use testing and opinion are included. Currently running nine issues a year, the cost is $24.97. It's best to call for latest subscription prices.

WOODCARVING

Marketshare Publications, Inc.
P.O. Box 11210
Shawnee Mission KS 66207

Information on this woodcarvers' title is to be available, but I don't currently have subscription prices. It appears to be a British import from the spellings and is said to be nicely done. Drop Marketshare a line to see what the magazine is really like.

WOODENBOAT MAGAZINE

P.O. Box 492
Mount Morris IL 61054-9852   (800) 877-5284

The above is the subscription department address setup, because this magazine is edited out of the same complex near Brooklin, ME that WoodenBoat Store, WoodenBoat Schools, and *Professional Boatbuilder* call home. I have only been there once but was very impressed with the dedication — no, it's more like an abiding interest, bordering strongly on love — that most of the people who work there have for the activity and their various interests that relate to that activity. The place is lovely, with old buildings put to what are now traditional uses. If you are interested in woodworking as it bears on making boats, whether it's building a ship's wheel or building a complete boat of wood, you must get this magazine. Recent stories covered making double-bladed paddles, as well as one of the series on the above-mentioned ship's wheel. Tool reviews also run, as do looks at historical wooden boats, balancing boat rigging, planking, wood technology, new designs, and an amazing amount of other material. Subscription price is currently $22.95 for a year of six issues.

WOODFIND

Box 2703
Lynnwood WA 98036

PC software that aids in the search for woodworking articles in a large number of woodworking publications. The free brochure describes the database and its uses, along with the ten magazines covered in 450+ issues.

WOODSHOP NEWS

35 Pratt St.
Essex CT 06426

An annual subscription price of $12.97 for six issues highlights this working wood shop newspaper, for serious amateurs and professionals alike. Check current subscription price before ordering.

WOODSMITH

Woodsmith Corporation
2200 Grand Ave.
Des Moines IA 50312   (800) 333-5075

Published bimonthly (six issues per year), *Woodsmith* offers plans, tips, and notes for a wide variety of projects. This is another older magazine, with almost fifteen years in business. The back issue I'm staring at right now has a super display cabinet project and also a sewing box. One large and complex, one small and moderate. The magazine tends to offer two, sometimes three or four, projects per issue, in almost exhaustive detail. In addition, there will be a number of tip articles and often a jig or two, all related to the main and subsidiary projects in some way. Tool tips are also offered, though seldom in the form of full-scale tests of tools. Like its companion *Shop Notes*, *Woodsmith* offers thirty-two pages of well done woodworking information, in a lush two-color format (brown is the second color, for a black and brown look that, on ivory paper, gives the magazine the appearance of a sepia-toned classic). The only advertising is a supplemental catalog in each issue, showing supplies for the projects featured in that issue. Usually this involves hardware, but may include formed plastic parts, tools (especially bits), books, binders, and so on. The supplement also

carries article material on making shelves, joints, etc., that makes them almost impossible to discard. A single year is $17.95 (call for the latest price information).

WOODTURNING

Marketshare Publications, Inc.
P.O. Box 11210
Shawnee Mission KS 66207

Information on this lathe lover's title is to be available, but I don't have current subscription prices. It appears to be a British import from the spellings and is said to be nicely done. Drop Marketshare a line to see what the magazine is really like. It is a companion magazine to *Woodcarving* and is the only general magazine devoted exclusively to wood turning.

WOODWORK

Ross Periodicals, Inc.
33 Redwood Dr.
P.O. Box 1529
Ross CA 94957   (415) 382-0580

Use the post office box address above for subscriptions to this bimonthly woodworking magazine of high quality. The magazine offers well-illustrated projects ranging from small boxes made in various interesting ways to larger projects — a nice-looking, easy to build daybed in the issue I have. There are tips, book reviews, and other departments to keep interest high. The subscription costs $17.00 per year, with instructional articles by Graham Blackburn one of the highlights of each issue.

WOODWORKER'S BOOK CLUB

P.O. Box 12171   Free information:
Cincinnati OH 45212-0171   (513) 531-8250

Each month brings a free issue of the club newsletter, describing the main selection and dozens of other selections. You have at least ten days to make up your mind. Drop a note to find out what the latest membership opening offer is. Currently, it's a free book plus a half-price book, with no obligation ever to buy another book, which is a great deal for any book club to offer. The club name describes the type of selections you'll find.

WOODWORKER'S BUSINESS NEWS

5604 Alameda Place NE
Albuquerque NM 87113   (800) 645-9292

The *Woodworker's Business News* is a monthly tabloid dedicated to helping small woodworking shops become more profitable. Press time subscription costs are $42 per year, but a free phone call can quickly update that information.

WOODWORKER'S JOURNAL

P.O. Box 1629
New Milford CT 06776   (203) 355-2694

The *Woodworker's Journal* is one of the oldest of top wood-working magazines, and it is definitely one of the top group. Currently in its sixteenth year, the magazine presents exceptionally interesting and well-designed projects covering a wide range of interests and skill levels. Drawings are nicely done, and photography is attractive and clear if not lush (I'd rather have attractive and clear in a magazine presenting do-it-yourself information). The six bimonthly issues cost $17.95 at press time.

WORKBENCH

KC Publishing, Inc.
700 West 47th St.
Kansas City MO 64112

Workbench is primarily a woodworking magazine but often includes other projects for around the house (shingling, drywall, and similar projects). Each issue contains several project articles, some easy, some complex. The issue I have in front of me offers four projects, two of which are medium to hard, and two of which are easy. All appear interesting, with good instructions and clear illustrations. The magazine is nicely done and has been around for a long time, almost fifty years. There are also tip departments, a problem solving department, and technique articles. *Workbench* also sells an extensive line of books and a large number of its own plans. Six issues per year (bimonthly), $12.95 annual subscription.

Videos

AAVIM

745-A Gaines School Rd.
Athens GA 30605   (706) 543-7557

The American Association for Vocational Instructional Materials is a non-profit developer, publisher, and distributor of instructional videos, books, and other resources, including computer software, for vocational students. Primarily, their customers are schools. On request, they'll send along a copy of their 90-page catalog, with woodworking educational materials described in the industrial education section. There are a lot of videos, with the cheapest being a project video, complete with a 22-page booklet. Shopsmith's series of woodworking videos is included in the list and is reasonably priced. Regardless of price, there are a fair number of videos and a couple of programs I'd love to own. Most come under the heading of "Maybe, someday," but you may find desires and wallet power that are stronger than mine. The Agriculture section includes some reasonably priced

materials on fence building, while the Construction Trades sections contain a lot of material on larger projects with wood. Tip: Get the manuals and forget the software unless you plan to teach classes.

VI-DAY-O PRODUCTIONS, INC.

Box 205
Palomar Mountain CA 92060-0205   (619) 548-7808

Richard Day is a former Home and Shop Contributing Editor for *Popular Science*, back in the days when it actually did that sort of publishing. He is the author of numerous do-it-yourself books on a variety of subjects and is now producing videotapes on everything from toilet replacement to birdhouse construction. Drop a note or give a call to get a copy of the current list of productions. It covers much more than woodworking subjects, and the tapes are well and conscientiously made.

VIDEO SIG

1030 East Duane Ave.
Sunnyvale CA 94086   (408) 730-9291

Call or write for a free catalog of instructional videos.

Associations and Guilds

AAVIM

745-A Gaines School Rd.
Athens GA 30605   (706) 543-7557

The American Association for Vocational Instructional Materials is a non-profit developer, publisher, and distributor of instructional videos, books, and other resources, including computer software, for vocational students. Primarily, their customers are schools. On request, they'll send along a copy of their 90-page catalog, with woodworking educational materials described in the industrial education section. (See listing on page 139.)

AMERICAN ASSOCIATION OF WOODTURNERS

667 Harriet Ave.
Shoreview MN 55126   (612) 484-9094

The AAW offers symposia on woodturning and is an international non-profit organization aimed at advancing woodturning. In essence, the Association provides information, education, and organization to those interested in lathe work, through a quarterly journal, *American Woodturner*, the membership directory, and other benefits, including the symposia. General membership is $25.00 annually. You may also contact them for dates and places of events.

AMERICAN PLYWOOD ASSOCIATION

P.O. Box 11700
Tacoma WA 98411-0700   (206) 565-6600

The APA Handy Plan catalog is $2.00 and lists and shows a wide variety of projects built primarily — naturally enough — of plywood in one form or another. The APA also offers many low cost booklets, brochures, and tech sheets that are of great help when larger projects loom, and plywood in large amounts and numbers of types must be bought. Ask about a listing of such technical bulletins.

CALIFORNIA REDWOOD ASSOCIATION

405 Enfrente Dr.
Suite 200
Novato CA 94949   (415) 382-0662

For a wide range of literature on types and uses of redwood lumber, the California Redwood Association can't be beat. The emphasis is on outdoor use, as one might expect, though I've found redwood makes an interesting material for large and small indoor projects as well. (I built two redwood bookshelves some time ago. They continue to stand in my dining room, where their appearance often draws comments because redwood is seldom used for such projects. Most indoor redwood projects are architectural, covering uses such as wall paneling and molding.) The Association's literature list offers everything from a Design-A-Deck plans kit to nail use information. Exterior and interior finishes are covered in large brochures, and there are pamphlets on the industry and its harvesting methods, and the environmental impact of using redwood. I'd suggest giving the Association a call or dropping them a note to request the literature list, at which time you can ask them about shipping costs that are added to literature prices on the list.

GUILD OF AMERICAN LUTHIERS

8222 S. Park Ave.
Tacoma WA 98408-5226   (206) 472-7853

The Guild presents the foremost magazine on musical instruments, and exhibits and other events are presented and listed. As the Guild describes itself: "a non-profit, tax-exempt educational organization, formed in 1972 to advance lutherie, the art and science of string instrument making and repair, through a free exchange of information." I don't have a great deal of interest in instrument making but must admit to fascination with some of the subjects covered in back issues of the quarterly magazine, including articles on cherry wood, working with koa, improving round-bottom planes, bending with rubber heat blankets, and much more. Members also get breaks on instrument plans and a good bit more for their annual $30.00.

SOUTHERN FOREST PRODUCTS ASSOCIATION

P.O. Box 52468
New Orleans LA 70152

SFPA is a good source for technical information on wood and its uses, emphasizing Southern pine, and provides a number of plans they call the "YouCanBuildIt" series, a series that grows with time. Plans are reasonable to low cost, and the plan list is #410, at a cost of $.30. Or you may ask for their catalog, with descriptions of literature and plans, ranging from permanent wood foundations to audiovisual material on softwood moisture content requirements.

WESTERN WOOD PRODUCTS ASSOCIATION

Yeon Building
522 S.W. Fifth Ave.
Portland OR 97204-2122

WWPA presents technical information on the species of wood their association emphasizes (Douglas fir, hem-fir, Engelmann spruce, Idaho white pine, lodgepole pine, sugar pine, Ponderosa pine, Western larch, Western cedars, and incense cedar), plus a good series of large and small plans at low cost. I'm looking at a plan for kid-sized storage modules now, their #62. It is easy to build and uses standard lumber sizes. Plan #61 is a mobile workbench that looks no harder to build. Drop a note asking for the current literature list or catalog of plans. The list is too long to reproduce here, but contains a good variety of plans that will almost certainly have one of interest to you.

WOODWORKING ASSOCIATION OF NORTH AMERICA

Box 667
Falmouth MA 02541-0667   (508) 548-2555

This is a show-presenting association, with single year dues of $25.00. Benefits include half-price admission to Woodworking World shows, free advice from a WANA tech consultant, bonus packets with project plans, and discount tool and supplies group purchase chances.

WOODWORKERS ALLIANCE FOR RAINFOREST PROTECTION

(WARP)
P.O. Box 133
Coos Bay OR 97420

Dedicated to the preservation of rain forest areas, WARP presents ideas for conservation and preservation of wood, aiming at sustainable development of all forest resources. Dues are $20.00 and bring a quarterly WARP journal.

THE WOODWORKING SHOWS

(800) 826-8267
(310) 477-8521

Call for a free brochure listing shows and dates. Shows are spread out, including Atlanta, Baltimore, Charlotte, Chicago, Dallas, Indianapolis, Kansas City, Milwaukee, San Diego, St. Louis, Tampa, and other areas. Call between 8 a.m. and 5 p.m., Monday through Friday, Pacific time.

This is an original Skilsaw. Things have changed, but not a whole lot, in over fifty years. Courtesy of Skil Corp.

About the Author

Charles Self is the author of more than thirty books, many on aspects of woodworking, including *101 Quick & Easy Woodworking Projects, Joinery: Methods of Fastening Wood,* and *Working with Plywood.* He has more than nine hundred magazine articles to his credit, for such magazines as *The Family Handyman, Popular Science, Workbench,* and *The Homeowner.* A member of the National Association of Home & Workshop Writers, he has served as consultant/copywriter for a number of major manufacturers. He lives in Bedford, Virginia.

The author beginning a turning for a book project.

Find It Fast Index

INDEX

A complete catalog of Betterway Books is available FREE by
writing to the address shown below, or by calling toll-free 1-
800-289-0963. To order additional copies of this book, send in
retail price of the book plus $3.00 postage and handling for
one book, and $1.00 for each additional book. Ohio residents
add 5½% sales tax. Allow 30 days for delivery.

Betterway Books
1507 Dana Avenue
Cincinnati, Ohio 45207